COVER LETTERS that KNOCK 'EM DEAD

COVER LETTERS *that* KNOCK 'EM DEAD

Martin Yate

Author of Knock 'em Dead with Great Answers to Tough Interview Questions and Resumes that Knock 'em Dead

BOB ADAMS, INC.
PUBLISHERS

Published by Bob Adams, Inc.
260 Center Street, Holbrook, MA 02343

ISBN: 1-55850-050-2

Printed in the United States of America

E   F   G   H   I   J

This publication is designed to provide accurate and authoritative information with regard to the subject matter covered. It is sold with the understanding that the publisher is not engaged in rendering legal, accounting, or other professional advice. If legal advice or other expert assistance is required, the services of a qualified professional person should be sought.
— From a *Declaration of Principles* jointly adopted by a Committee of the American Bar Association and a Committee of Publishers and Associations.

Other books by Martin Yate . . .

Knock 'em Dead: The Ultimate Job Seeker's Handbook
The all-new edition of Martin Yate's classic now covers the entire job search. The new edition features sections on: where the jobs are now and where they will be tomorrow (and how to best approach the companies that have them); keeping the financial boat afloat; how to recharge a stalled job hunt; "safety networking" to protect your job and career regardless of the economy; the electronic edge—why corporate resume databases and electronic bulletin boards are the new wave for the career-savvy; and bridging the gender gap in salary negotiation. Of course, this new edition also features Yate's famous great answers to tough interview questions—and time-tested advice on salary negotiations, dealing with executive search firms, illegal interview questions, and drug testing. $6\frac{1}{16}$ x $9\frac{1}{4}$ inches; 312 pages, paperback, $7.95.

Resumes that Knock 'em Dead
Every single one of the 110 resumes in this book is based on a resume that was successfully used to obtain a job. Many of the resumes included were used to change careers; others resulted in dramatically higher salaries. Some produced both. Yate reviews the marks of a great resume, what type of resume is right for each applicant, what always goes in, what always stays out, and why. $8\frac{1}{2}$ by 11 inches; 216 pages, paperback, $7.95.

Hiring the Best: How to Staff Your Department Right the First Time (3rd ed.)
Contrary to popular belief, not all managers are mystically endowed with the ability to hire the right people. Interviewing is a skill that must be developed, and Martin Yate shows just how to identify the person who provides the best "fit" for any given position. Includes sections on interviewing within the law and hiring clerical help, as well as prewritten interview outlines. 6 x 9 inches; 204 pages, paperback, $9.95.

If you cannot find a book at your local bookstore, you may order it directly from the publisher. Please send payment including $3.75 for shipping and handling (for the entire order) to: Bob Adams, Inc., 260 Center Street, Holbrook, MA 02343. Credit card holders may call 1-800-USA-JOBS (in Massachusetts, 617-767-8100). Please check your local bookstore first.

To good fortune
the intersection of opportunity,
preparation, and effort

READ THIS FIRST

THERE'S A CRUEL PARADOX AT WORK WHEN IT COMES TO WRITING COVER LETTERS. We strive to excel in our professions, spending our energies to become top-notch accountants, truck drivers, brain surgeons . . . and we spend little or no time learning to promote ourselves on the printed page. When suddenly our livelihood depends on our ability to compose a compelling written summary of the advantages of working with us, we find ourselves in dire straits.

If we ever developed the necessary skills in school, we find they have long since rusted. Writing it all down for review by others in a position to hire us has simply never made it onto the daily to-do list. Many professionals create the thoughts behind their business communications, but hire others to craft (and not always well) the messages themselves.

If you find yourself in this situation at the most inopportune time imaginable—during your job search—take heart. This book will solve your problem quickly. Use it exactly as I recommend in the pages that follow. If you do, you will reap a number of benefits, the most important of which is this:

- Your job hunt and ensuing career will benefit tremendously, because your letters will look great, pack a punch, get read, and position you as a mover and shaker worth interviewing.

There are other advantages:

- You won't waste a moment of precious time.
- You'll have the satisfaction of having made a tough, intricate, and vitally important professional challenge a little easier and more enjoyable than it is for most people in your shoes (your competitors, for example).
- You might even have some fun.

❏ ❏ ❏

Employers go through four distinct stages in reaching a hiring decision.

1. Long list development. Advertising and other sources develop the biggest possible field of qualified candidates.

2. Short list development. The long list is screened to rule out also-rans. Those who make the cut are invited in for an interview.

3. Short list prioritization. Through a series of two or three interviews, candidates are weeded out. Those still standing are ranked according to various criteria.

4. Short list review. After the dust settles, each candidate's strengths and weaknesses are reviewed for one last time before the final decision. The information in the dossier created for every short-list candidate plays a key role here.

In each of these steps, letters have a role to play in taking you to the next level. For example, a resume without a cover letter rarely gets any further than the trash can. A "To Whom It May Concern" letter fares little better.

It's estimated that the average piece of business correspondence gets less than thirty seconds of the reader's attention. Even a truly great cover letter will not get much more. In crafting your cover letter, you are not aiming to win a place next to a favorite novel on the reader's bedside table. You are out to win that *momentary flash of genuine interest* and get your cover letter read with something like serious attention. Once that's accomplished, you can use the models for the follow-up letters in this book to help you a step upward on the four-tiered ladder to the job offer.

Letters help you move through each phase of the hiring cycle and on to the offer in ways most people have never understood. In the fourth step, the short list review, the interviewer recalls what happened in each phase of the interview cycle. All notes and documentation in the applicant dossier are reviewed on each candidate. This means that *as you pass through each step of the cycle, you are presented with a heaven-sent opportunity to advance your candidacy when The Moment of Truth finally arrives.* You can forward all manner of pertinent information that will identify you as the unquestioned prime choice when that last, most critical evaluation is taking place.

❑   ❑   ❑

I took a common-sense approach to putting this book together: I collected over 4,000 successful job-hunting letters from the most cynical professionals in the country, corporate human resource people and professional headhunters. I approached over a thousand of these people and asked them to provide the truly impressive letters they came across—the letters that made a difference, grabbed attention, and advanced someone's candidacy against tough competition. The cream of the crop can be found within these covers.

From these letters, and from my discussions with professionals in the field, I learned about certain things that work and don't work when putting together a cover letter. These are explored in detail later on in the book, but there is one overriding factor that virtually all the successful letters shared. It's worth exploring here.

All but a handful of the letters were only one page long. Yours probably should be, too. Why is brevity so important? My sources feel that:

1. They don't have time to wade through dense patches of text, and they view those who can't get to the point in a dim light.

2. Second pages get detached and often lack sufficient contact information. (For that matter, first pages often fall short in the same category.)

Perhaps the most overlooked benefit of a comprehensive mail dimension to your job-hunting campaign is that the letters can be working for you while you are investing your time and energy elsewhere. A strong mail dimension to your plan can double and triple your effectiveness.

If you use the letters simply as noncustomized templates, you may open a few doors. But the real you will be so different from the letters that the interviewers will eventually be left with a nagging doubt that you aren't all you appear to be.

Browse through the letters in the second half of this book. Not all of them will fit your needs at this moment, but take a look anyway. You will see, on every page, proven methods of getting the good word across to potential employers.

This book will also highlight key phrases and wording techniques that caught the eyes of people whose eyes are usually tough to catch. Eventually, you will want to incorporate these into your own letters.

In choosing the examples for this book, I was pleased to see that the ones that rose to the top were all businesslike, with no gimmickry or "cuteness.". Some may even seem a little dry to you, but remember: they worked. This collection of successful job-hunting letters includes the best of the best as determined by corporate gatekeepers and captains of industry who know a winner when they see one. It is just such people who will be evaluating your efforts, and the drawbridge of opportunity will be raised (or lowered) for you depending on their evaluation.

Now let's learn how to put together some jigsaw puzzles. I suggest that you read this book with a highlighter in hand, so as to be able to flag appropriate sections for later reference. That way you'll have a wealth of good ideas you can use after just one read. Then you'll be ready to create your own unique job-hunting letters that will knock 'em dead.

TABLE OF CONTENTS

CHAPTER ONE:

WHAT IS A COVER LETTER?

DO YOU EVER RECEIVE JUNK MAIL? We all do. what do you do with the stuff marked "occupant"? You junk it—either without reading it, or after a quick glance. Junk mail never gets the attention a personal letter does.

Too many employment queries end up being treated as junk mail—and if a piece of correspondence is treated like junk mail, that's what it is. Your cover letter is the personalized factor in the presentation of an otherwise essentially impersonal document, your resume. A good cover letter sets the stage for the reader to accept your resume as something special. Only if your cover letter and resume do their job will interviews and job offers result.

When the envelope is opened, your cover letter is the first thing seen. It can make an indelible first impression. Of course, I'm not saying that the letter alone will get you the job, or even land you the interview, but it *will* help you along the way by getting that resume read with something like serious attention.

The higher up the professional ladder you climb, the more important cover letters and job hunting letters become. For the candidate who must demonstrate written communication skills in the execution of daily duties (and that's just about all of us), these letters become a valuable vehicle for demonstrating critical job skills. Mess up here and the door to opportunity could well slam shut.

Step One

Grab your reader's ATTENTION. Do this by using quality typesetting, stationery, and envelopes. If you don't have personal stationery use the same paper your resume is printed on. This way your letter and resume will match and give an impression of balance and continuity. See the chapter entitled "The Final Product" for details.

Step Two

Generate INTEREST with the content. Do this by addressing the letter to someone by name and quickly explaining what you have to offer. The first sentence grabs attention, the rest of the paragraph gives the reader the old one-two punch. The rule is: Say it strong, say it straight and don't pussy-foot.

Do some research. Even a little can get your letter off to a fast start. Case in point:

> "I came across the enclosed article in *Newsweek* magazine and thought it might interest you. It encouraged me to do a little research on your company. I am now convinced of two things: You are the kind of people I want to be associated with; and I have the kind of qualifications you can use."

Of course, in the real world, we can't all apply for jobs with companies that are featured in the big magazines. Here are some more everyday examples.

> "I have been following the performance of your fund in Mutual Funds Newsletter. The record over the last three years shows strong portfolio management. With my experience working for one of your competitors, I know I could make significant contributions . . ."

> "Recently I have been researching the local _____ industry. My search has been for companies that are respected in the field and that provide ongoing training programs. The name _____ keeps coming up as a top company.

> "With the scarcity of qualified and motivated *(your desired job title)* that exists today, I felt sure that it would be valuable for us to talk."

> "Within the next few weeks I will be moving from New York to _____ . Having researched the companies in my field in my new home town, I know that you are the people I want to talk to . . ."

> "The state of the art in _____ changes so rapidly that it is tough for most professionals to keep up. I am the exception. I am eager to bring my experience to bear for your company."

Step Three

Now turn that INTEREST into DESIRE. First, tie yourself to a specific job category or work area. Use phrases like:

> "I am writing because . . ." or "My reason for contacting you . . ."

> ". . . should this be the case, you may be interested to know . . ."

"If you are seeking a _____, you will be interested to
know . . ."

"I would like to talk to you about your personnel needs and
how I am able to contribute to your department's goals."

"If you have an opening for someone in this area, you will
see that my resume demonstrates a person of unusual dedication, efficiency and drive."

Next, call attention to your merits with a short paragraph that highlights one or two of your special contributions or achievements:

"I have an economics background from Columbia and a quantitative analysis approach to market fluctuations. This
combination has enabled me consistently to pick the new
technology flotations that are the backbone of the growth-
oriented mutual fund."

Similar statements applicable to your area of expertise will give your letter more per-sonal punch. Include any qualifications, contributions, and attributes that prove you are someone with plenty of talent to offer. If an advertisement (or a conversation with a poten-tial employer) reveals an aspect of a particular job opening that is not addressed in your resume, it should be covered in your cover letter:

"I notice from your advertisement that audio and video
training experience would be a plus. In addition to the
qualifications stated in my enclosed resume, I have over
five years of experience writing and producing sales and
management training materials in both these media."

Whether you use bullets, or list your achievements in short staccato sentences will be determined in part by the amount of space available to you on the page.

Step Four

Here's where you letter turns that DESIRE into ACTION. The action you're shooting for is that the reader will dash straight on to your resume, then call you in for an interview. You achieve this action with brevity—leave the reader wanting more.

Make it clear to the reader that you want to talk. Explain when, where, and how you can be contacted. You can now be *pro-active* by telling the reader that you intend to follow up at a certain point in time if contact has not been established by then. The reader may then want to initiate action himself.

Just as you worked to get the opening right, labor over the closing. It is the reader's last remembrance of you; make it strong, make it tight and make it obvious that you are serious about entering into meaningful conversation.

Useful phrases include:

"It would be a pleasure to give you more information about
my qualifications and experience . . ."

15

"I look forward to discussing our mutual interests further . . ."

"While I prefer not to use my employer's time taking personal calls at work, with discretion I can be reached at _____ . . ."

"I will be in your area around the 20th, and shall call you prior to that date. I would like to arrange . . ."

"I hope to speak with you further and will call the week of _____ to follow up."

"The chance to meet with you would be a privilege and a pleasure, so to this end I shall call you on _____."

"I look forward to speaking with you further and will call in the next few days to see when our schedules will permit a face-to-face meeting."

"May I suggest a personal meeting where you can have the opportunity to examine the person behind the resume."

"My credentials and achievements are a matter of record that I hope you will examine in depth when we meet . . ."

"I look forward to examining any of the ways you feel my background and skills would benefit *(name of organization)*. I look forward to hearing from you."

"Resumes help you sort out the probables from the possible, but they are no way to judge the caliber of an individual. I would like to meet you and demonstrate that I have the personality that makes for a successful _____."

"I expect to be in your area on Tuesday and Wednesday of next week and wonder which day would be best for you. I will call to determine." (As many employed people are concerned about their resumes going astray you may wish to add: "In the meantime, I would appreciate my application being treated as confidential, as I am currently employed.")

"With my training and hands-on experience, I know I can contribute to _____, and want to talk to you about it in person. When may we meet?"

"After reading my resume, you will know something about my background. Yet you will still need to determine whether I am the one to help with the current problems and challenges. I would like an interview to discuss my ability to contribute."

"You can reach me at _____ to arrange an interview. I
know that your time investment in meeting with me will be
amply repaid."

". . . Thank you for your time and consideration; I hope to
hear from you shortly."

"May I call you for an interview in the next few days?"

"A brief phone call will establish whether or not we have
mutual interest. Recognizing the demands of your schedule,
I will make that call within the week."

As we have noted, some people feel it is a powerful closing to state a date—"I'll call you on Friday if we don't speak before"—or a date and time—"I'll call you on Friday morning at 10 am if we don't speak before." The logic is that you demonstrate that your intent is serious, that you are organized, and that you plan your time effectively (all desirable behavioral traits).

On the other hand, at least one "authority" has said that the reader would be offended by being "forced" to sit and await your call. Frankly, in twenty years of being involved in the hiring process, I have never felt constrained by such statements; I guess I'm just not the sensitive type. What I look for is the person who *doesn't* follow through on commitments as promised. If you use this approach, keep your promises.

CHAPTER TWO:

TYPES OF COVER LETTERS

The General Cover Letter

HERE IS AN EXAMPLE OF A GENERAL COVER LETTER. It has been created using the example phrases from earlier in this book (note the highlighted text). You too can write a dynamite cover letter with a word processor by using the old "cut and paste" technique. Then all you have to do is make the minor adjustments necessary to personalize each document. (This letter should be sent as a result of direct research.)

JAMES SHARPE

18 Central Park Street   ◆   Anytown, NY 14788
(516) 555-1212

Jackson Bethell, V.P. Operations   October 2, 19—
Link Products
621 Miller Drive
Anytown, CA 01234

Dear Jackson Bethell,

Recently I have been researching the leading local companies in data communications. My search has been for companies that are respected in the field and who provide ongoing training programs. The name of DataLink Products keeps coming up as a top company.

I am an experienced voice and data communications specialist with a substantial background in IBM environments. If you have an opening for someone in this area you will see that my resume demonstrates a person of unusual dedication, efficiency, and drive.

My experience and achievements include:

- The complete redesign of a data communications network, projected to increase efficiency company-wide some 12 percent.

- The installation and troubleshooting of a Defender II call-back security system for a dial-up network.

I enclose a copy of my resume, and look forward to examining any of the ways you feel my background and skills would benefit DataLink Products. While I prefer not to use my employer's time taking personal calls at work, with discretion I can be reached at (213)555-1212 to initiate contact. Let's talk!

Yours truly,

James Sharpe

Here is an example using a different selection of phrases. The letter is designed for use in response to an advertisement.

JANE SWIFT

18 Central Park Street, Anytown, NY 14788
(516) 555-1212

David Doors, Director of Marketing   January 14, 19—
Martin Financial Group
1642 Rhode Island Way
Anytown, NY 01234

Dear David Doors,

I have always followed the performance of your fund in Mutual Funds Newsletter.

Recently your notice regarding a Market Analyst in INVESTORS DAILY caught my eye—and your company name caught my attention because your record over the last three years shows exceptional portfolio management. Because of my experience with one of your competitors, I know I could make significant contributions.

I would like to talk to you about your personnel needs and how I am able to contribute to your department's goals.

An experienced market analyst, I have an economics background (MS Purdue) and a strong quantitative analysis approach to market fluctuations. This combination has enabled me to consistently pick the new technology flotations that are the backbone of the growth-oriented mutual fund. For example:

I first recommended ABC Fund six years ago. More recently my clients have been strongly invested in Atlantic Horizon Growth (in the high-risk category), and ABC Growth and Income (for the cautious investor). Those following my advice over the last six years have consistently outperformed the market.

I know that resumes help you sort out the probables from the possible, but they are no way to judge the personal caliber of an individual. I would like to meet and demonstrate that along with the credentials, I have the personality that makes for a successful team player.

Yours truly,

Jane Swift

The Executive Briefing

Here is a variation on the traditional cover letter. Called an executive briefing, this kind of letter gets right to the point and makes life easy for the corporate recruiter. Only those who read the *Knock 'em Dead* books know of this technique.

Why send an executive briefing? It's often the weapon of choice because:

1. The initial resume screener might have little understanding of the job or its requirements.

2. Your general resume invariably needs customizing for any specific job. (Overly broad resumes are like "one-size-fits-all" clothes—one size usually fits none.)

3. Your resume is somewhat (or more than somewhat) out of date and you have to send *something* out immediately to take advantage of the opportunity of a lifetime.

Also worth considering: resume screeners like people who make life a little easier for them.

Based on my extensive experience on both sides of the desk, I developed the executive briefing to increase the odds of your resume getting through to the right people.

How can the executive briefing help you through the screening and multiple interview cycle? To answer this we must begin by acknowledging a painful fact. Your resume, by definition, has drawbacks. It is usually too general to relate your qualifications to each

20

specific job. More than one person will probably be interviewing you, and when this happens, the problems begin.

A manager says, "Spend a few minutes with this candidate and tell me what you think." Your general resume may be impressive, but the manager rarely adequately outlines the job being filled or the specific qualifications he or she is looking for. This means that other interviewers do not have any way to qualify you fairly and specifically. While the manager will be looking for specific skills relating to projects at hand, the personnel department will be trying to match your skills to the vagaries of the job-description manual, and the other interviewers will flounder because no one told them what to look for. A chain of events like this, naturally, could reduce your chances of landing a job offer.

The executive briefing, which supplements the resume, solves this problem with its layout. It looks like this:

JAMES SHARPE

18 Central Park Street, Anytown, NY 14788
(516) 555-1212

Dear Sir/Madam:

While my resume will provide you with a general outline of my work history, my problem-solving abilities, and some achievements, I have taken the time to list your current specific requirements and my applicable skills in those areas.

Your Requirements	My Skills
1. Management of public reference, etc.	1. Experience as head reference librarian at University of Smithtown.
2. Supervision of 14 full-time support employees.	2. Supervised support staff of 17.
3. Ability to work with larger supervisory team in planning, budgeting, and policy formation.	3. During my last year I was responsible for budget and reformation of circulation rules.
4. ALA-accredited MLS.	4. ALA-accredited MLS.
5. 3 years' experience.	5. 1 year with public library; 2 with University of Smithtown.

You will see that my attached resume provides further in-depth background. I hope this will enable you to use your time effectively today.

Sincerely,

James Sharpe

An executive briefing sent with a resume provides a comprehensive picture of a thorough professional, plus a personalized, fast, and easy-to-read synopsis that details exactly how you can help with an employer's current batch of problems.

The executive briefing assures that each resume you send out addresses the job's specific needs and that every interviewer at that company will be interviewing you for the same job.

The use of an executive briefing is naturally restricted to jobs you have discovered through your own efforts or seen advertised. It is obviously not appropriate when the requirements of a specific job are unavailable.

The Broadcast Letter

The broadcast letter is a simple but effective variation on the cover letter. Much of the information will be culled from your resume, as the intent of the Broadcast Letter is to *replace* the resume. You would be well advised here to conduct an in-depth analysis of your background in much the same way you would for a resume (see chapter 4). A broadcast letter can often get you into a telephone conversation with a potential employer, but that employer is usually likely to request a proper resume before seeing you anyway.

You should also know that broadcast letters are most frequently used by mature, successfully established professionals.

Beware: if you don't *have* a resume, you might well have to fill out one of those dreadful application forms. This requires putting your background in the format the employer wants—not the package of your choice. Consequently, I do not advise using this kind of letter as the spearhead or sole thrust of your campaign. Rather, you should use it as an integral part of the campaign in one of these ways:

- For small, highly targeted mailings to specific high-interest companies, where it works as an effective customizing technique.

- For small, highly targeted mailings to specific high-interest jobs about which you have enough detailed knowledge that such a letter would supersede the effectiveness of your resume.

- As an initial thrust, but with the more traditional cover letter and resume already in place for a back-up second mailing. In practice, the cold-mailed broadcast letter often results in a request for a resume and other times results in a telephone interview and subsequent invitation to a face-to-face interview—with the request that you bring a resume.

- As part of a multiple-contact approach where you are approaching a number of people within a company with personalized letters (see chapter 6).

- As a back-up approach when your cover letter and resume don't generate the response you want from individual target companies.

- To headhunters. Broadcast letters rarely get passed on to employers without your permission.

Here is what a typical Broadcast Letter might look like.

JANE SWIFT

---

18 Central Park Street, Anytown, NY 14788   ■   (516) 555-1212

Dear Employer,

For the past seven years I have pursued an increasingly successful career in the sales profession. Among my accomplishments I include:

SALES
As a regional representative, I contributed $1,500,000, or 16 percent, of my company's annual sales.

MARKETING
My marketing skills (based on a B.S. in marketing) enabled me to increase sales 25 percent in my economically stressed territory, at a time when colleagues were striving to maintain flat sales. Repeat business reached an all-time high.

PROJECT MANAGEMENT
Following the above successes, my regional model was adopted by the company. I trained and provided project supervision to the entire sales force. The following year, company sales showed a sales increase 12 percent above projections.

The above was based and achieved on my firmly held zero price discounting philosophy. It is difficult to summarize my work in a letter. The only way I can think of for providing you the opportunity to examine my credentials is for us to talk with each other. I look forward to hearing from you.

Yours sincerely,

Jane Swift

Employment Agencies and Executive Recruiters

You might as well know something about headhunters right from the get-go. The best way to get the attention of headhunters is to give them the respect they deserve. They are, after all, the most sophisticated salespeople in the world—they and they alone sell products that talk back!

A headhunter will be only faintly amused by your exhortations "to accept the challenge" or "test your skills by finding me a job" in the moments before he or she practices hoops with the remains of your letter and the trash can. They don't have the time or inclination to indulge such whimsical ideas. So with headhunters—whether they are working for the local employment agency, contingency, or retained search firm—bear these two rules in mind and you won't go far wrong:

1. Cut to the chase.

2. Tell the truth. Answer questions truthfully and you will likely receive help. Get caught in a lie and you will have established a career-long distrust with someone who possesses very diverse and influential list of contacts.

> "I am forwarding my resume, as I understand you specialize in representing clients in the _____ field."

> "Please find the enclosed resume. As a specialist in the _____ field, I felt you might be interested in the skills of a _____."

> "Among your many clients may be one or two who are seeking a position as a _____."

Remember that in a cover letter to executive search firms and employment agencies you should mention your salary and, if appropriate, your willingness to relocate.

Here is an example of a cover letter you might send to a corporate headhunter:

James Sharpe

18 Central Park Street, Anytown, NY 14788   ■   (516) 555-1212

Dear Mr. O'Flynn:

As you may be aware, the management structure at _____ will be reorganized in the near future. While I am enthusiastic about the future of the agency under its new leadership, I have elected to make this an opportunity for change and professional growth.

My many years of experience lend themselves to a management position in any medium-sized service firm, but I am open to other opportunities. Although I would prefer to remain in Detroit, I would entertain other areas of the country, if the opportunity warrants it. I am currently earning $65,000 a year.

I have enclosed my resume for your review. Should you be conducting a search for someone with my background, at the present time or in the near future, I would greatly appreciate your consideration. I would be happy to discuss my background more fully with you on the phone or in a personal interview.

Very truly yours,

James Sharpe

CHAPTER THREE:

WHAT GOES IN, WHAT STAYS OUT

ONCE UPON A TIME, THERE WERE JUST A FEW SET RULES FOR WRITING A GREAT JOB-HUNTING LETTER. Everything was black and white—you did this, you didn't do that. The rules of the game have changed; now more than ever, communication is a prerequisite for any job.

Saying "I'm a great engineer. Give me a chance and I'll prove it to you" just doesn't cut it any more. It is no longer economically feasible to take employees on approval. Today job skills and behavioral traits are under close scrutiny throughout the entire selection process. Make no mistake; the process starts the moment you make contact—and that means the content and style of your cover letter had better be up to snuff.

If there is one overriding objective for your cover and follow-up letters, it is to *demonstrate your awareness and possession of the learned behavioral traits that make for successful professionals and good hires.*

Developing Personal, Professional, Achievement, and Business Profiles

There are twenty universally admired key personality or behavioral traits; they are your passport to success in all aspects of your job hunt. When reading your letter, the interviewer will search for clues to determine what kind of person you really are. The presence of positive clues in your letter tells the company representative how you feel about yourself and your chosen career, and what you will be like to work with.

Personal Profile

Use these words and phrases to project a successful, healthy personal profile.

Drive: A desire to get things done. Goal-oriented.

Motivation: Enthusiasm and a willingness to ask questions. A company realizes a motivated person accepts added challenges and does that little bit extra on every job.

Communication
Skills: More than ever, the ability to talk and write effectively to people at all levels in a company is a key to success.

Chemistry: The company representative is looking for someone who does not get rattled, wears a smile, is confident without self-importance, and gets along with others—in short, a team player.

Energy: Someone who always gives that extra effort in the little things as well as more important matters.

Determination: Someone who does not back off when a problem or situation gets tough.

Confidence: With every level of employee—neither intimidated by the big enchiladas nor overly familiar.

Professional Profile

All companies seek employees who respect their profession and employer. Projecting these professional traits will identify you as loyal, reliable and trustworthy.

Reliability: Following up on yourself, not relying on anyone else to ensure the job is done well, and keeping management informed every step of the way.

Honesty/
Integrity: Taking responsibility for your actions, both good and bad. Always making decisions in the best interest of the company, never on whim or personal preference.

Pride: Pride in a job well done. Always taking the extra step to make sure the job is done to the best of your ability. Paying attention to the details.

Dedication: Doing whatever it takes in time and effort to see a project through to completion, on deadline.

Analytical Skills: Weighing the pros and cons. Not jumping at the first possible solution to a problem. Being able to weigh the short- and long-term benefits of a solution against all its possible negatives.

Listening Skills: Listening and understanding, as opposed to waiting your turn to speak.

Achievement Profile

Companies have very limited interests: making money, saving money (the same as making money), and saving time, which does both. Projecting your achievement profile, in however humble a fashion, is the key to winning any job.

Money Saved: Every penny saved by your thought and efficiency is a penny earned for the company.

Time Saved: Every moment saved by your thought and efficiency enables your company to save money and make more in the additional time available. Double bonus.

Money Earned: Generating revenue is the goal of every company.

27

Business Profile

Projecting your business profile is important on those occasions when you cannot demonstrate ways you have made money, saved money, or saved time for previous employers. These keys demonstrate you are always on the lookout for opportunities to contribute and that you keep your boss informed when an opportunity arises.

Efficiency: Always keeping an eye open for wastage of time, effort, resources, and money.

Economy: Most problems have two solutions: an expensive one and one that the company would prefer to implement.

Procedures: Procedures exist to keep the company profitable. Don't work around them. This means keeping your boss informed. Tell *your* boss about problems or good ideas, and don't go over his or her head. Follow the chain of command. Do not implement your own "improved" procedures or organize others to do so.

Profit: The reason all the above traits are so universally admired in the business world is that they relate to profit.

Your goal is to draw attention to as many of these traits as possible by direct statement, inference, or illustration.

Writing a job-hunting letter is a bit like baking a cake. In most instances the ingredients are essentially the same—what determines the flavor is the order and quantity in which those ingredients are blended. There are certain ingredients that go in almost every letter, whether cover, broadcast, network, follow-through, acceptance, rejection, or resignation letters. There are others that rarely or never go in, and there are those special touches (a pinch of this, a smidgin of that) that may be included depending on your personal tastes and the need the letter will satisfy.

Brief Is Beautiful

Advertisements and job hunting letters have a great deal in common. You will notice that the vast majority of advertisements in any media can be heard, watched, or read in under thirty seconds—the upper limit of the average consumer's attention span.

It is no coincidence that both cover letters and resumes depart from the rules that govern all other forms of writing. Like commercials, they need to be absorbed in less than thirty seconds. First and last they are an urgent business communication, and business likes to get to the point.

Before putting pen to paper, good copywriters imagine themselves in the position of their target audience. They know their objective: to sell something. Then they consider what features their product possesses and what benefits it can confer on the purchaser. This invariably requires some understanding of the target or targets.

For the next fifteen minutes, imagine yourself in one of your target companies. You are in the personnel department on "screening" detail. Fortunately, it is a slow morning and there are only thirty resumes and accompanying cover letters that need to be read. Go straight to the example sections of this book now and read thirty examples without a break, then return to this page.

❏   ❏   ❏

Now you have some idea of what it feels like, except that you had it easy. The letters you read were good, interesting ones—letters that got real people real jobs. Even so, you probably felt a little punch drunk at the end of the exercise. But I know that you learned a very valuable lesson: *Brevity is beautiful.* Can you imagine what it might be like to do this every day for a living?

The first thing you have to do is understand why some people get hired over others. Then look at your own background in a way that will enable you to get your point across. Every hire is made on a job applicant's ability to satisfy these five concerns of the employer:

1. Ability and suitability.

2. Willingness to go the extra yard, to take the rough with the smooth.

3. Manageability, taking direction and constructive input in a positive and professional manner.

4. Problem-solving attitude.

5. Supportive behavioral traits.

A Question of Money

Advertisements often request salary information. With the right letter you will rarely be denied at least a telephone conversation, even if you do omit your salary history. Nevertheless, there may be factors that make you feel obliged to include something. I have heard recently that some personnel people consider the word "negotiable" annoying, though perhaps not grounds for refusing to see an applicant.

If you choose to share information about salary, it must go on the cover letter or be attached to the cover letter. It should never go on the resume itself. If you choose not to include it, the contact can always ask you. When *desired salary* is requested, don't restrict yourself to one figure; instead, give yourself a range with a spread between the low and the high end. This dramatically increases your chances of "clicking onto" the available salary range.

When *salary history* is requested, the prospective employer is usually looking for a consistent career progression. Gaps or significant cuts could raise red flags. If you have nothing to hide and have a steadily progressive earnings history, spell it out on a separate sheet.

Many of us have less than perfect salary histories for any number of perfectly valid reasons. Consequently, we don't want to release these figures unless we are there in person to explain away the seeming anomalies. In these instances the matter is best skirted in the cover letter itself.

Here is one way to address the topic of money in your letters should you feel it is appropriate to do so. You will find others later in the book.

```
"My salary is in the mid $ _____ s, with appropriate
benefits. I would be willing to relocate for the right op-
portunity."
```

Telephone

Once you have determined a primary contact number (and that shouldn't be too difficult) you must ensure that it will be answered at all times. There is no point in mounting a job-hunting campaign if prospective and eager employers can never reach you. Invest in an answering machine (about $50) or hiring an answering service (between $30 to $75 a month). If your choice is an answering machine, keep the message businesslike. Once recorded, call the machine from another phone. Are you impressed?

You also need an alternate number; if at all possible, it should be answered by someone who is just about always there (perhaps a family member).

Ingredients: A Basic Checklist

As you read through the letters in Chapter 7, bear in mind that for your letters to be effective, they must:

- Address a person, not a title . . . and whenever possible, a person who is in a position to make a hiring decision.

- Be tailored to the reader as far as is practical, to show that you have done your homework.

- Show concern, interest, and pride for your profession; demonstrate energy and enthusiasm.

- Cut to the chase.

- Avoid stuffiness, and maintain a balance between professionalism and friendliness.

- Include information relevant to the job you are seeking.

- Ask for the next step in the process clearly and without either apology or arrogance.

Finally, notice the variety of letters for every job-hunting situation that you can craft to maximize both the volume and value of your offers.

CHAPTER FOUR:

ASSEMBLING YOUR COVER LETTER

THERE IS A FINE LINE BETWEEN PRIDE OF ACHIEVEMENT AND INSUFFERABLE ARROGANCE. To help you focus on experiences and behaviors in your work life that will help advance your candidacy, complete this questionnaire. Answer the questions for each of your jobs, starting with the most recent and working backward.

Take some time over this exercise and go back carefully over past jobs. Your answers to this questionnaire will form the meat and potatoes for your letters. It isn't going to be necessary to craft knock 'em dead sentences from scratch, although (believe it or not) you could, given the time and commitment. With the help of this book you'll be able to cut and paste with the best of them—your end result being a unique and arresting letter.

However, the parts of your constructed letter that will be entirely original will be those areas that address your contributions and achievements. That means you need to spend adequate time in this period of preparation. What you jot down here will later be crafted into punchy sentences.

Questionnaire

FOR EACH OF YOUR PREVIOUS JOBS:
List three to five major duties:

_____

_____

_____

_____

_____

This questionnaire was taken from the comprehensive "Skills Analysis" questionnaire in *Resumes that Knock 'em Dead*. Completion of this comprehensive evaluation tool will reward the prudent professional.

FOR EACH OF THESE DUTIES:
What special skills or knowledge did you need to perform these tasks satisfactorily?

_____

_____

_____

What was the biggest problem you faced in this area?

_____

_____

_____

What was your solution, and the result of the solution?

_____

_____

_____

What was your biggest achievement in this area? Think about money made or saved or time saved for the employer.

_____

_____

_____

What verbal or written comments did your peers or managers make about your contributions in this area?

_____

_____

_____

What was the greatest contribution in this area you made as a team player?

_____

_____

_____

```
What desirable behavioral traits did you call on in this area
to get the job done?
```

_____

_____

_____

Now that you've completed the questionnaire, it's time to put your responses to work for you.

Creating Punchy Sentences

Concise, punchy sentences grab attention.

The most grammatically correct sentences in the world won't get you interviews (except perhaps as a copy editor—and then not always) because such prose can read as though every breath of life has been squeezed out of it.

Sentences gain power with verbs that demonstrate an action. For example, one professional—with a number of years at the same law firm in a clerical position—had written:

```
"I learned to use a Wang 220VS."
```

Pretty ordinary, right? Well, after discussion of the circumstances that surrounded learning how to use the Wang 220VS, certain exciting facts emerged. By using action verbs and an awareness of employer interests, this sentence was charged up and given more punch. Not only that, but for the first time the writer fully understood that value of her contributions, which greatly enhanced her self-image:

```
"I analyzed and determined the need for automation of an
established law office. I was responsible for hardware and
software selection, installation, and loading. Within one
year I had achieved a fully automated office. This saved
forty hours a week."
```

Notice how the verbs show that things *happened* when she was around the office. These action verbs and phrases add an air of direction, efficiency and accomplishment to every cover letter. They succinctly tell the reader what you did and how well you did it.

Rewrite each of your query answers using action verbs to punch them up. To help you in the process, here are over 180 action verbs and phrases you can use.

accomplished	approved	built
achieved	arranged	calculated
acted	assembled	catalogued
adapted	assigned	chaired
addressed	assisted	clarified
administered	attained	classified
advanced	audited	coached
advised	authored	collected
allocated	automated	compiled
analyzed	balanced	completed
appraised	budgeted	composed

33

computed
conceptualized
conducted
consolidated
contained
contracted
contributed
controlled
coordinated
corresponded
counseled
created
critiqued
cut
decreased
delegated
demonstrated
designed
developed
devised
diagnosed
directed
dispatched
distinguished
diversified
drafted
edited
educated
eliminated
enabled
encouraged
engineered
enlisted
established
evaluated
examined
executed
expanded
expedited
explained
extracted
fabricated
facilitated
familiarized
fashioned
focused
forecast
formulated
founded
generated

guided
headed-up
identified
illustrated
implemented
improved
increased
indoctrinated
influenced
informed
initiated
innovated
inspected
installed
instituted
instructed
integrated
interpreted
interviewed
introduced
invented
investigated
launched
lectured
led
maintained
managed
marketed
mediated
moderated
monitored
motivated
negotiated
operated
organized
originated
overhauled
oversaw
performed
persuaded
planned
prepared
presented
prioritized
processed
produced
programmed
projected
promoted
provided

publicized
published
purchased
recommended
reconciled
recorded
recruited
reduced
referred
regulated
rehabilitated
remodeled
repaired
represented
researched
restored
restructured
retrieved
reversed
reviewed
revitalized
saved
scheduled
schooled
screened
set
shaped
skilled
solidified
solved
specified
stimulated
streamlined
strengthened
summarized
supervised
surveyed
systematized
tabulated
taught
trained
translated
traveled
trimmed
upgraded
validated
worked
wrote

Varying Sentence Structure

Good writers are at their best writing short punchy sentences. You will see that if the letters in Chapter 7 have any single thing in common, it's punchy sentences. Keep your sentences under about twenty words; a good average is around fifteen. If your sentence is longer than the twenty mark, change it. Either shorten it by restructuring or make two sentences out of one. The reader on the receiving end has neither the time nor the inclination to read your sentences twice to get a clear understanding. However, you will want to avoid choppiness. Try to vary the length of sentences when you can.

You can also start with a short phrase ending in a colon:

- Followed by bullets of information.

- Each one supporting the original phrase.

All of these techniques are designed to enliven the reading process. An example follows.

```
Analyzed and determined need for automation of an estab-
lished law office:
```
- Responsible for hardware and software selection.

- Coordinated installation of Wang 220VS and 6 work sta-
tions.

- Operated and maintained equipment; trained other users.

- Full automation achieved in one year.

- Savings to company: $25,000.

K.I.S.S. (Keep It Simple, Stupid)

Just as you use short sentences, use common words. They communicate quickly and are easy to understand. Stick to short, simple words whenever possible (without sounding infantile). Of course, you need action words and phrases—but the key is to stay away from obscure words.

Communicating, persuading, and motivating your readers to take action is challenging because many people in different companies will see your letters and make judgments based on them. This means you must keep industry "jargon" to a minimum (especially in the initial contact letters—covers, broadcast, and the like). There will be those who understand the intricacies and technicalities of your profession—but unfortunately, many of the initial screeners do not. They won't know the niceties of your particular job, and you'll need to share your specialist wisdom with the non-specialists first, before you can expect to reach your professional peers.

Short words for short sentences help make gripping short paragraphs:
good for short attention spans!

Within your short paragraphs and short sentences, beware of name and acronym dropping, such as "I worked for Dr. A. Witherspoon in Sys. Gen. SNA 2.31." This is a good way to confuse (and lose) readers. Such statements are too restricted to have validity outside the small circle of specialists to whom they speak. Unless you work in a highly technical field, avoid them. Your letters demand the widest possible appeal, yet they need to remain personal in tone. (Of course, you don't want your missives to sound like they're from Publishers' Clearing House, either.)

Voice and Tense

The voice you develop for different letters depends on a few important factors:

- Getting a lot said in a small space.
- Being factual.
- Packaging yourself in the best way.
- Using what feels good to you.

The voice you use in your letters should be consistent throughout. There is considerable disagreement among the "experts" about the best voice, and each of the following options have both champions and detractors.

Sentences in all types of cover letters can be truncated (up to a point), by omitting pronouns such as *I, you, he, she, it, they, a,* or *the*:

```
"Automated office."
```

In fact, many authorities recommend the dropping of pronouns as a technique that both saves space and allows you to brag about yourself without seeming boastful. It gives the impression of another party writing about you.

Others feel that to use the personal pronoun—"I automated the office..."—is naive, unprofessional, and smacks of boasting. These experts suggest you use the third person:

```
"S/he automated the office."
```

Of course, just about the only way you are likely to use the third person in a letter is when you are attributing quotes about you to a third party.

At the same time, some experts recommend that you write in the first person because it makes you sound more human.

```
"I automated the office."
```

In short, there is no hard and fast rule here—they can all work given the many unique circumstances you will face in any given job hunt. Use whatever style works best for you. If you do use the personal pronoun, try not to use it in every sentence—it gets a little monotonous, and with too much use, it can make you sound like an egomaniac. The mental focus is not "I" but "you," the person with whom you are trying to communicate.

A nice variation is to use a first-person voice throughout the letter and then a final few words in the third person. Make sure these final words appear in the form of an attributed quote, as an insight to your value:

```
"She managed the automation procedure and we didn't ex-
perience a moment of down time."
                        - Jane Ross, Department Manager
```

Don't mistake the need for professionalism in your job hunting letters with stiff-necked formality. The most effective tone is one that mixes the conversational and the formal, just the way we do in our offices and on our jobs. The only overriding rule is to *make the letter readable*, so that the reader can see a human being shining through the pages. You will notice from the examples in chapter 7 that the personality of the writer comes right through.

Length

If you are writing an early draft in longhand it can be difficult to judge how it will convert to typescript. As a general rule of thumb, two pages of double spaced handwriting usually make one page of typescript. Whatever you do, don't listen to the bozos who tell you to use handwritten cover letters. Occasionally under special circumstances, follow-up letters may be handwritten (for example, if you are out of town and using hotel stationery), but never initial contact letters.

The accepted rule for length is usually one page for a cover letter. Subsequent letters stemming from verbal communications—whether over the telephone or face-to-face—should also ideally adhere to the one-page rule, but can run to two pages if complexity of content demands it. Generally speaking, no job hunting letter should exceed two pages. Break this rule at your peril; to do so will brand you as a windbag incapable of getting to the point. Not the kind of person who gets a foot in the door!

Having said this, I should acknowledge that all rules are made to be broken. Occasionally a three-page letter might be required, but *only* in the following two instances:

1. You have been contacted directly by an employer about a specific position and have been asked to present data for that particular opportunity.

2. An executive recruiter who is representing you determines that the exigencies of a particular situation warrant a dossier of such length. (Often such a letter and resume will be prepared exclusively—or with considerable input—by the recruiter.)

You'll find that thinking too much about length considerations while you write will hamper the process. Think instead of the story you have to tell, then layer fact upon fact until your tale is told. Use your words and the key phrases from this book to craft the message of your choice. When *that* is done you can go back and ruthlessly cut it to the bone.

Ask yourself these questions:

- Can I cut out any paragraphs?
- Can I cut out any sentences?
- Can I cut out any superfluous words?
- Where have I repeated myself?

If in doubt, cut it out—leave nothing but facts and action words! If at the end you find too much has been cut, you'll have the additional pleasure of reinstating your deathless prose.

Your Checklist

There are really two proofing steps in the creation of a polished cover letter. You do the first at this point, to make sure that all the things that should be in are—and that all the things that shouldn't aren't. The final proof is done before printing or typesetting and is discussed later in the book.

Warning: It is easy, in the heat of the creative moment, to miss crucial components or mistakenly include facts that give the wrong emphasis. Check all your letters against these points:

Contact information

● The pertinent personal data (name, address, zip code, and personal telephone number) is on every page.

● Your business number is omitted unless it is absolutely necessary and safe to include it.

● If your letter is more than one page long, each page is numbered "page 1 of 2," etc. and all the pages are stapled together so that they cannot get separated or mislaid. Remember the accepted way of stapling business communications: one staple in the top left-hand corner.

Objectives

● Does your letter state why you are writing? To apply for a job, follow up on an interview, etc.?

● Is the letter tied specifically to the target company and job (if you have details)?

● Does it address points of relevance, such as skills that apply from the ad or agenda items addressed at the interview?

● Does it include references to some of your personality or behavioral traits that are crucial to success in your field?

● Is your most relevant and qualifying experience prioritized to lend strength to your letter?

● Have you avoided wasting more space than required with employer names and addresses?

● Have you omitted any reference to reasons for leaving a particular job? Reasons for change might be important to the employer at the interview, but they are *not* relevant at this point. Use this precious space to sell, not to justify.

● Unless they have been specifically requested, have you removed all references to past, current or desired salaries?

● Have you removed references to your date of availability? Remember, if you aren't available at their convenience, why are you wasting their time by writing?

● If your education is mentioned, is it relevant to the advertisement?

● Is your highest educational attainment the one you mention?

● Have you avoided listing irrelevant responsibilities or job titles?

● Have you mentioned your contributions, your achievements, and the problems you have successfully solved during your career?

● Have you avoided poor focus by eliminating all extraneous information? ("Extraneous" means anything that doesn't relate to your job objective, such as captaining the tiddlywinks team in kindergarten.)

- Is the whole thing long enough to whet the reader's appetite for more details, yet short enough not to slake that thirst?

- Have you left out lists of references and only mentioned the availability of references (if of course, there is nothing more valuable to fill up the space)? To employers this is a given. If you aren't prepared to produce them on demand, you simply won't get the job.

- Have you let the obvious slip in, like heading your letter "Letter of Application" in big bold letters? If so, cut it out.

Writing Style

- Substitute short words for long words, and one word where previously there were two.

- Keep your average sentence ten to twenty words. Shorten any sentence of more than twenty words or break it into two sentences.

- Keep every paragraph under five lines, with most paragraphs shorter.

- Make sure your sentences begin with or contain, wherever possible, powerful action verbs and phrases that demonstrate you as a mover and shaker.

- If you are in a technical field, weed out as much of the jargon as possible. As we have seen, this is most important in cover letters and broadcast letters; they are likely to be screened by non-techies. Part of their job is to try to assist in the hiring of techies who can communicate with the rest of the human race. In subsequent letters to fellow techies, however, the technical jargon may not only be desirable; it may be mandatory to get your point across.

CHAPTER FIVE:

THE FINAL PRODUCT

STYLE—SO EASY TO SEE BUT SO DIFFICULT TO DEFINE—USUALLY HAS A DISTINCT LOOK AND FEEL. Here are some of the basics you should keep in mind when creating stylish and professional job-hunting letters.

Typing and Layout

The average cover letter arrives on a desk along with as many as fifty or sixty others, all of which require screening. You can expect your letter to get a maximum of thirty seconds of attention, and that's only if it's accessible to the reader's eye.

The biggest complaints about job-hunting letters that kamikaze into the trash can in record time are:

- They have too much information crammed into the space and are therefore hard on the eyes.

- Amateurish typing.

- The layout is unorganized, illogical and uneven. (In other words, it looks shoddy and slapdash—and who wants an employee like that?)

- Misspellings and visibly corrected spellings.

Typewriter or Computer

If you plan to be employable in the year 2000, you'd better wake up and smell the coffee—computer literacy is a must. Typing on typewriters doesn't cut it any more. Typing your letter or using a typing service is the equivalent of carving your job hunting letters in tablets of stone. It looks old-fashioned, and it must be done from start to finish every time you need to send it to someone else or customize it for another purpose. If you cannot now prepare your letters on a computer, engage the services of a good word processing outfit while you get up to speed.

The crucial difference between typing on a typewriter and word processing on a computer is the computer's ability to store information on a disk. This means that every letter can be immediately customized for every different job. A word processing service will give you free (or very cheap) changes in these instances. You can target endless variations of your letters to fit the special nuances of all the different jobs you come across in your search.

Once stored on disk, your entire series of job hunting letters is ready for updating as long as you live. Logic and the short odds say that some fine day you will use these letters again. Hold onto the disks.

Hard copy

With a computer, the printing unit is separate from the box that does the actual word processing. Is that important? Yes, because just as all typewriters are not created equal, neither are all printers; and while printers are not the business end of the machine, they are the end that business sees! When you use a computer printer or a word processing service, insist on your letters being printed on a letter quality printer or a laser printer; either of these will give you high quality print. You must never accept what is known as dot matrix, thermal, or Near Letter Quality (NLQ) printers because they lack the razor sharpness you need. *Don't let anyone tell you otherwise—ever.*

If you use thermal, dot matrix or near letter quality printers *IT COULD COST YOU THE JOB*, today or next year. The reason: companies are increasingly adopting new scanning technology, allowing a computer to look at a letter or resume (through a copier-type peripheral) and store the data in memory. So a growing number of companies will be storing your communications not on paper but on disk. Many scanners are incapable of reading the output of NLQ, thermal and dot matrix printers.

Typefaces/fonts

If you are using a laser printer, remember—you don't have to use those boring old pica and elite typefaces that scream "typewriter." A laser printer gives you a vast choice of print styles and quality fonts. Business is rapidly coming to accept the likes of Bookman, New York, and Palatino as the norm, and these typefaces are only available through laser printer output or professional typesetting. By the way, when choosing your type face, stay away from heavy and bold for your body copy (although you may choose to take a more dramatic approach with key words or headlines). Bold type takes up too much space, and if it needs to be copied on the receiving end, it can blur and look dreadful. Avoid "script" faces similar to handwriting; while they look attractive to the occasional reader, they are harder on the eyes of the person who reads any amount of business correspondence. Capitalized copy is tough on the eyes too; we tend to think it makes a powerful statement when all it does for the reader is cause eye strain.

How to Brighten the Page

Once you decide on a typeface, stick with it. More than one font on a page can look confusing. You can do plenty to liven up the visual impact of the page within the variations of the typeface you have chosen.

Most typefaces come in a selection of regular, bold, italic, and bold italic. Good job hunting letters will take judicious advantage of this: you can vary the impact of key words with italics, underlined phrases, and emboldened or capitalized titles for additional emphasis. There are a lot of options.

You will notice from the occasional example in this book that letters will use more than one typographical variation of the same font. For example, a writer who wants to emphasize personality traits might italicize only those words or phrases that describe these aspects. That way the message gets a double fixing in the reader's mind. You will also notice powerful letters that employ no typographic pyrotechnics and still knock 'em dead! In the end, it's your judgment call.

If you are crafting letters that are general in content, you will need to use (or have your word processing service use) the mail merge feature of the word processing program. What this does is fill in the blanks: "Dear _____" becomes "Dear Fred Jones." What you must watch out for is someone putting the merged words in a different typeface or format.

```
Dear Jack Jones:
Your January 11, 1990 ad in the Chicago Tribune described a
need for an accountant.
```

All this does is state loud and clear that this is a form letter sent, in all likelihood, to hundreds. Why needlessly detract from your chances of being taken seriously?

Another no-no for the computer literate is the use of "clip art" to brighten the page. Those little quill pens and scrolls may look nifty to you, but they look amateurish to the rest of the business world.

Choosing a Word Processing Service

A word or two of special advice is in order here. Small companies come and go with great rapidity, so when your cover letter is finished, ask for three copies of it on disk. Why three? Funny things can happen to disks (I once lost half a book because of disk malfunction). Consequently, everyone with a computer should always maintain two back-up copies of the original document; *each on a separate disk*, making a total of three copies. This way, no matter where you find yourself living next time your career demands a job hunt, your letters are ready for updating. By the way, you should not be charged more than a couple of dollars for each back-up disk. Even the best quality disks only cost about $1, and the copying process takes maybe 60 seconds to complete. Negotiate the cost of the copies before you assign the project; that way you won't have the unpleasantness of any unscrupulous operator trying to take advantage of you. (Helpful hint: Be sure the label on the disk identifies the software environment in which the letters were composed.)

Typesetting

A step up from laser printing is the professional typesetting option. If you choose this, the quality of type appearing in your cover letter will be of the level found in most books, magazines, and newspapers. It is superior to that produced by any home printer, although the gap is narrowing rapidly, and no one, even now, has been known to object to laser quality.

Typesetting Services

All the guidelines for choosing word processing services also apply to typesetting services. There are regular typesetters and those that have a side specialty in resumes and cover letters; the latter is naturally your best choice. There are also any number of local newspapers around the country that do resume typesetting as a sideline. They charge between $25 to $45.

Proofing

It simply isn't possible for even the most accomplished professional writer to go from draft to print, so don't try it. Your pride of authorship will hide blemishes you can't afford to miss.

You need some distance from your creative efforts to give yourself detachment and objectivity. There is no hard and fast rule about how long it should take to come up with the finished product. Nevertheless, if you think you have finished, leave it alone at least overnight. Then come back to it fresh. You'll read it almost as if it were meeting your eyes for the first time.

Before you have your letters typed or printed, make sure that your writing is as clear as possible. Three things guaranteed to annoy cover letter readers are incorrect spelling, poor grammar, and improper syntax. Go back and check all these areas. If you think syntax has something to do with the IRS, you'd better get a third party involved. An acquaintance of mine came up with an eminently practical solution. She went to the library, waited for a quiet moment, and got into a conversation with the librarian, who subsequently agreed to give her letter the old once-over. (Everyone loves to show off special knowledge!)

The quality of paper always makes an impression on the person holding the page. The folks receiving your letter see literally dozens of others every day, and you need every trick available to make your point. The heft of high-quality paper compared to the shining-thru copying paper sends an almost subliminal message about certain personality traits (notably attention to detail). Another reason for using high-quality paper for your copies is that it takes the ink better, giving you clean, sharp print resolution.

By the way, if an emergency demands you send a letter by fax, remember to follow it up with a copy on regular paper. This is because everything you send is likely to end up in your "candidate dossier," and thermal fax paper will yellow and curl in no time flat. A fax can also obliterate important parts of any communication.

While you should not skimp on paper costs, neither should you buy or be talked into the most expensive available. Indeed, in some fields (health care and education come to mind), too ostentatious a paper can cause a negative impression. The idea is to create a feeling of understated quality. You can get 500 sheets of excellent paper for about $20 in most areas of the country.

As for color, white is considered to be the prime choice. Cream is also acceptable, and I'm assured that some of the pale pastel shades can be both attractive and effective.These pastel shades were originally used to make letters and resumes stand out. But now everyone is so busy standing out of the crowd in Magenta and Passionate Puce that you just might find it more original to stand out in white or cream. White and cream are straightforward, no-nonsense colors. They say BUSINESS.

It is a given that cover letter stationery should always match the color and weight of your envelopes and resume. To send a white cover letter—even if it is your personal stationery—with a cream resume is gauche and detracts from the powerful statement you are trying to make. In fact, when you print the finished letter, you should print some letterhead sheets at the same time and in the same quantity. It should be in the same typeface and on the same kind of paper. You don't need to get too fancy; base your design on other stationery you've been impressed with. With the advent of word processing, it takes less than thirty minutes to create.

Likewise, all subsequent letters should be on the same paper. Your written communication will be filed. Then, prior to the hiring decision, the hiring manager will review all the data on all the short list candidates; your coordinated written campaign will paint the picture of a thorough professional. The sum of your letters will be more powerful as a whole simply because there will be continuity of form and content.

Envelopes Send Messages Too

What goes on the envelope affects the power of the message inside. Over the last six months I've asked a number of line managers and Human Resource professionals how the envelope's appearance affected the likelihood of the letter being read and with what kind of anticipation. Here's what I heard:

```
"I never open letters with dot matrix printed pressure sen-
sitive labels; I regard them as junk mail and I simply don't
have the time in my life for ill-targeted marketing at-
tempts."

"I never open anything addressed to me by title but not by
name."

"I will open envelopes addressed to me by misspelled name,
but I am looking with a jaundiced eye already; and that eye
is keen for other examples of sloppiness."

"I always open correctly typed envelopes that say personal
and/or confidential, but if they're not, I feel conned. I
don't hire con artists."

"I always open neatly handwritten envelopes. What's more, I
open them first, unless there's another letter that is ob-
viously a check."
```

There are those who recommend enclosing a stamped addressed envelope to increase the chances of response. You can do this, but don't expect many people in the corporate world to take advantage of your munificence. I have never known this tactic to yield much in the way of results. On the whole I think you are better advised to save the stamp money and spend it on a follow-up telephone call; conversations lead to interviews. I have never heard of a single interview being set up exclusively through the mails.

(*Neat trick department:* I recently received an intriguing resume and cover letter; both had attached to the top right hand corner a circular self-adhesive red spot. It worked as a major exclamation point; I was impressed. I was even more impressed when I realized that once this left my hands no other reader would know exactly who attached the spot, but they *would* pay special attention to the content because of the spot. Nice technique; don't let the whole world in on it, though.)

Appearance

Remember, that first glance and first feel of your letter can make a powerful impression. Go through this checklist before you seal the envelope:

- Does the paper size measure 8½" by 11", and is it of good quality, between 16 and 25 lbs. in weight?
- Have you used white, off-white, or cream-colored paper?

- Did you make sure to use only one side of the page?

- Is your name, address, and telephone number on every page?

- If more than one page, have you paginated your cover letter: "1 of 2" at the bottom of the page and so on?

- Are the pages stapled together? Remember, one staple in the top left-hand corner is the accepted protocol.

CHAPTER SIX:

THE PLAN OF ATTACK

GREAT COVER, BROADCAST, AND FOLLOW-UP LETTERS WON'T GET YOU A JOB BY SITTING ON YOUR DESK LIKE RARE MANUSCRIPTS. You have to do something with them.

Even a company with no growth rate can still be expected (based on national averages) to experience a 14 percent turnover in staff in the course of a year. In other words, every company has openings *sometime*, and any one of those openings could have your name on it.

The problem is, you won't have the chance to pick the very best opportunity unless you check them all out. Every intelligent job hunter will use a five-tiered approach to cover all the paper bases, including:

- Newspaper advertisements.

- Personal and professional networking.

- Direct researched opportunities.

- Employment agencies and recruiters.

- Business and trade publications.

An intelligent and comprehensive campaign will embrace all these approaches.

Help-wanted Advertisements

A first step for many is to go to the want ads and do a mass mailing. Bear in mind, there should be a method to your madness when you do this. Remember, if it is the first idea that comes to *your* mind, hitting the want ads will be at the front of everyone else's thoughts, too.

A single help-wanted advertisement can draw hundreds of responses. The following ideas might be helpful:

- Most newspapers have an employment edition every week (usually Sunday, although sometimes mid-week), when, in addition to their regular advertising, they have a major drive for help-wanted ads. Make sure you always read this edition of your local paper.

- So-called "authorities" on the topic will tell you not to rely on the want ads—

that they don't work. Rockinghorse droppings! Want ads don't work only if you are too dumb to know how to use them. Look for back issues. Just because a company is no longer advertising does not necessarily mean that the slot has been filled. The employer may well have become disillusioned—and is now using a professional recruiter to work on the position. They may have filled the position; perhaps the person never started work or simply didn't work out in the first few months. Maybe they hired someone who *did* work out and now they want another one. When you go back into the want ads you'll find untold opportunities awaiting you, and instead of competition from 150 other job hunters responding to this Sunday's want ad there may be just one or two people vying for the slot.

I had a letter from a *Knock 'em Dead* reader recently who told me he had landed a $90,000 job from a seven-month-old want ad he came across in a pile of newspapers in his father-in-law's garage! (You see? There is a use for in-laws, after all.)

- In many instances jobs are available but just aren't being advertised. It's what the press refers to as the hidden job market. Likewise, in some high-demand occupations where want ads aren't famous for drawing the right caliber of professional, the employer may only run one or two major "institutional" ads a year for that type of position.

- Cross-check the categories. Don't rely solely on those ads seeking your specific job title. For example, let's say you are a graphic artist looking for a job in advertising. You should flag all advertising or public relations agencies with any kind of need. If they are actively hiring at the moment, logic will tell you that their employment needs are not restricted to that particular title.

If you are writing as the result of a newspaper advertisement, you should mention both the publication and the date. Do not abbreviate advertisement to "ad" unless space demands, and remember to underline or italicize the publication's title:

```
"I read your advertisement in the Daily Gotham on October 6th
and, after researching your company, felt I had to write . . ."

"I am responding to your recent advertisement offering the
opportunity to get involved with _____."

"In re: Your advertisement in the Columbus Dispatch on Sun-
day the 8th of November. As you will notice, my entire back-
ground matches your requirements."

"Your notice regarding a _____ in _____ caught my
eye, and your company name caught my attention."
"This letter and attached resume is in response to your ad-
vertisement in _____."
```

Networking

Networking is one of those dreadful words from the seventies that unfortunately is so entrenched we might as well learn to live with it. Strip the hyperbole and it just means communicating with everyone you can get hold of: professional colleagues, academic peers, or personal contacts, whether you know them well or not.

I must admit my attitude toward networking among professional colleagues and personal friends has undergone a change. In earlier times I pooh-poohed the idea as a copout employed by the weak-willed. I said the only way to go was to bite the bullet, pick up the telephone, and make contact. This is still the fastest and most effective way. But I now recognize that for a job hunt to be most effective, direct mail has an important part to play. Even so, I still harbor fears that someone, once comfortable with networking among old friends, will unconsciously derail a job hunt by ignoring other and possibly more fruitful avenues of exploration for job opportunities. You would be wise to harbor the same fears; an effective job hunt is more than writing to and shooting the breeze with old cronies on the telephone.

What made me change my opinion? I consciously began to track my responses to requests for job hunting assistance.

To those requests from people I didn't know, I asked for a resume. If I received it in good time with a thoughtfully prepared accompanying letter, I would give that person help if I could.

To those requests from people with an introduction from someone I liked and respected, I gave time and consideration and, wherever possible, assistance.

To those requests from friends, people I had worked with at one time and *who had kept in touch* since we had worked together, I stopped everything and went through my Rolodex. I provided leads, made calls on their behalf, and insisted they keep in touch. I also initiated follow-up calls myself on behalf of these people.

To those requests from people who regarded themselves as friends but who had *not* maintained contact, or who had only re-established contact when they wanted something, I looked through the Rolodex once but for some reason was unable to find anything. I wished them the best of luck. "Sorry I couldn't help you. If something comes to mind I'll be sure to call."

Nothing works like a personal recommendation from a fellow professional—and you get that best by *being* a fellow professional. It is no accident that successful people in all fields know each other—they helped each other get that way.

If you are going to use business colleagues and personal friends in your job hunt, don't mess up and do it half-heartedly. We live in a very mobile society, so you shouldn't restrict yourself to family, friends and colleagues just where you are looking. Everyone can help—even Aunt Matilda in Manila: maybe she just happens to have had her cousin's wife's husband, who is a senior scientist at IBM, as her house guest for a month last summer and he is now forever in her debt for the vacation of a lifetime. Maybe not, but still, people know people, and they know people not just here but all over. Sit and think for a few minutes; you will be amazed at the people *you* know all over the country. Every one of them has a similar network.

Here are some tips for writing letters asking for assistance. If you feel awkward writing a letter to certain contacts, use these guidelines as a basis for the telephone conversation you'll have instead.

1. Establish connectivity. Recall the last memorable contact you had or someone in common that you have both spoken to recently.

2. Tell them why you are writing: "It's time for me to make a move; I just got laid off with 1,000 others and I'm taking a couple of days to catch up with old friends."

3. Ask for advice and guidance: "Who do you think are the happening

_____ companies today?" "Could you take a look at my resume for me? I really need an objective opinion and I've always respected your viewpoint." Don't ask specifically, "Can you hire me?" or "Can your company hire me?"

4. Don't rely on a contact with a particular company to get you into that company. Mount and execute your own plan of attack. No one has the same interest as you for putting bread on your table.

5. Let them know what you are open for. They will invariably want to help, but you have to give them a framework within which to target their efforts.

6. Say you hope you'll get to see each other again soon or "one of these days." Plan on doing something together. Invite them over for drinks, dinner, or a barbecue.

7. When you do get help, say thank you. And if you get it verbally, follow it up in writing. The impression is indelible, and just might get you another lead.

8. You never know who your friends are. You will be surprised at how someone you always regarded as a real pal won't give you the time of day and how someone you never thought of as a friend will go above and beyond the call of duty for you.

9. Whether they help you or not, let them know when you get situated, and maintain contact in one form or another at least once a year. A career is for a long time. It might be next week or a decade from now when a group of managers (including one of your personal network) are talking about filling a new position and the first thing they will do is say "Who do we know?" That could be you . . . if you establish "top of the mind awareness" now and maintain it.

If you are writing as the result of a referral, say so and quote the person's name if appropriate:

"Our mutual colleague, John Stanovich, felt my skills and abilities would be valuable to your company . . ."

"The branch manager of your San Francisco branch, Pamela Bronson, has suggested I contact you regarding the opening for a _____."

"I received your name from Henry Charles last week. I spoke to Mr. Charles regarding career opportunities with _____ and he suggested I contact you. In case the resume he forwarded is caught up in the mail, I enclose another."

"Arthur Gold, your office manager and my neighbor, thought I should contact you about the upcoming opening in your accounting department."

Direct Research Contacts

Most companies are listed in one of the reference sources in your library. Take the time to do library research and you will discover job opportunities that 90 percent of your professional competitors never dream exist. The business reference section can give you access to numerous research books that can help:

- Standard and Poors
- The Directory of Directories
- State Directory of Manufacturers
- Contacts Influential
- The National Job Bank

Again, the reference librarian will be pleased to help you. Search each of the appropriate reference works for every company within the scope of your search that also falls within your geographic boundaries.

Your goal is to identify and build personalized dossiers on the companies in your chosen geographic area. Do not be judgmental about what and who they might appear to be: you are fishing for possible job openings, so cast your net wide and list them all. Only if you present yourself as a candidate for all available opportunities in your geographic area of search is there any realistic chance of landing the best possible opportunity.

Unfortunately, no single reference work is ever complete. Their very size and scope means that most are at least a little out of date at publication time. Also, no single reference work lists every company. Because you don't know what company has the very best job for you, you need to research as many businesses in your area as possible, and therefore you will have to look through numerous reference books.

Take a pad of paper, and using a separate sheet for each company, copy all the relevant company information onto that piece of paper. You'll want to include the names of the company's president and chairman of the board, a description of the complete lines of company services and/or products, the size of the company, and the locations of its various branches. Of course, if you find other interesting information, copy it down, by all means. For instance, you might come across information on growth or shrinkage in a particular area of a company; or you might read about recent acquisitions the company has made. Write it all down.

All this information will help you target potential employers and stand out in different ways. Your knowledge will create a favorable impression when you first contact the company; that you made an effort is noticed and sets you apart from other applicants who don't bother. The combination says that you respect the company, the opportunity, and the interviewer; combined, these perceptions help say that you are a different quality of job candidate.

All your effort has an obvious short-term value in helping you with job interviews and offers. Who would *you* interview and subsequently hire? The person who knows nothing about your company, or the person who knows everything and is enthusiastic about it?

Your effort also has value in the long term, because you are building a personalized reference work of your industry/specialty/profession that will help you throughout your career whenever you wish to make a job change.

Purchasing Mailing Lists

Purchasing mailing lists from professional mailing list companies can be cheap and effective. Chances are there is a mailing list of exactly the kinds of movers and shakers you want to work for. These lists can be broken down for you by title, geography, zip code—all sorts of ways. They are affordable, too; usually about $100 for a thousand addresses. To contact a broker, just look in your yellow pages under "mailing list brokers/compilers."

If you want the most comprehensive source catalog, call the Direct Marketing Association at (212)768-7277. Ask for the publications department; for $30 you can get the List Brokerage Directory. This is the single most comprehensive source of mailing lists available. With compilation specialists in every conceivable area, this directory can certainly lead you towards the right list.

As we have noted, even the most up-to-date lists and directories are out of date by the time they get to you, so it is a good investment of time to call and verify that Joe Schmoe, VP of Engineering, is still there. Apart from the obvious goal of sending mail to the right person, if Joe is no longer there you may be able to find out where he went. If so, you'll have uncovered another opportunity for yourself.

(Note: Mailing lists can be effective, but be sure to read the envelopes section in chapter 5 before you purchase pre-printed mailing labels.)

Associations

You're a member of an appropriate professional association, aren't you? Of course you are—or, if not, you will want to invest in membership just as soon as humanly possible. You don't know of an appropriate association? Your local research librarian will gladly lead you to an enormous blue and yellow tome published by Bowker called *The Encyclopedia of Associations*; your gang will be listed there.

When you join an association, you get a membership roster with which you can network amongst your peers. This is the modern day equivalent of the "old boy" and "old girl" network. Also, for a nominal sum you can often pick up a pre-printed mailing list or the same on disk to use with your word processor. (However, before you splurge on pre-printed mailing labels, read about envelopes in chapter 5.)

Alumni Associations

Many schools have an active alumni association. The mailing list you can obtain from this source can vary from just names to names and occupations and (sometimes) names of employers. Being a fellow alumni probably gives you claim to sixty seconds of attention. Nearly every working alumni could be worthy of a networking letter (just check through the examples) and a follow-up call. Never ever underestimate the power of "the old school tie."

Employment Agents

There are essentially three categories: State employment agencies, private employment agencies, and executive recruiters.

State Employment Agencies

These are funded by the state labor department and typically carry names like State Employment Security, State Job Service, or Manpower Services. The names may vary, but the services remain the same; they will make efforts to line you up with appropriate jobs and mail resumes out on your behalf to interested employers who have jobs listed with them. It is not mandatory for employers to list jobs with state agencies, but more and more are taking advantage of these free services. Once the bastion of minimum-wage jobs, positions listed with these public agencies can now reach $50,000 to $60,000 a year for some positions.

If you are moving across the state or across the country, your local employment office can plug you into what is known as a national job bank, which theoretically can give you access to jobs all over the nation. However, insiders agree that it can take up to a month for a particular job from a local office to hit the national system. The most effective way to use this service is to visit your local office and ask for an introduction to the office in your destination area. Then send them a cover letter with your resume and follow up with a phone call.

Private Employment Agency Sources

The following are a few sources for employment service listings, from temporary help, through local employment agency, contingency, and retained headhunters. Depending on who you are and what you are looking for, any or all of these categories could be of interest to you. Here is some contact data for the most comprehensive lists and directories available.

National Association of Personnel Consultants
1432 Duke Street
Alexandria, VA 22314
(703)684-0180
National Directory of Personnel Consultants, $19.95. Identifies companies by occupational specialization and geographical coverage. Includes employment agencies, contingency, and retained search companies in membership. The industry's premier organization, with thousands of reputable contacts.

Directory of Executive Recruiters
Kennedy & Kennedy Inc.
Templeton Road
Fitzwilliam, NH 03447
(603)585-2200.
Directory of Executive Recruiters, $39.95.
Details on 2,000 retained and contingency firms throughout North America.

National Job Campaigning Resource Center
Box 9433
Panama City Beach, FL 32417
(904)235-3733
Ken Cole is the president of this organization, which should be known as Legwork Central. The company provides many of the research services offered by the top outplacement firms, but it is supported by the individual consumer. Among its unique and exciting job-hunting products are:

101 industry-specific directories of top contingency and retained search firms throughout the U.S. These are updated quarterly and provide pinpoint accuracy for just $9.00 a directory. A great deal.

Executive Research Directory. $78. This is a tremendous resource for the senior-level executive. Perhaps you need firms engaged in the development of artificial intelligence. This directory provides you with the resources who can track this information down for you and save you the legwork.

Senior Executive Research Package. $125. Includes the Executive Research Directory and a printout of the 400 research directors at many of the nation's leading search firms.

National Association of Temporary Services
119 South St. Asaph Street
Alexandria, VA 22314
(703)549-6287

A self-addressed stamped envelope with a polite request will get you a free listing of temporary help companies in the state of your choice. A full listing of 7,300 firms is available for $135. The information is also available on disk; ask for prices.

Don't restrict yourself to any single category in this area. Executives, especially, should not turn their nose up at local employment agencies. Often a local agency has better rapport and contacts with the local business community than the big name search firm. I have also known more than one "employment agency" that regularly placed job candidates earning in excess of $250,000 a year. Don't get hung up on agency versus search firm labels without researching the firms in question; you could miss some great opportunities.

Business Magazines

There are a number of uses here. The articles about interesting companies can alert you to growth opportunities, and the articles themselves can provide a neat little entree in your cover letter. Most professional trade magazines rely more or less on the contributions of industry professionals. So articles bylined by Nate Sklaroff, vice president of Openings at Sesame Furnaces, could go into a little dossier for strictly targeted mailings. It's also a neat idea to enclose the clipping with your letter. These mailings to sometime authors can be tremendously rewarding. Writing is hard and writers have egos of mythical proportions (just ask my editor). A little flattery can go a long way.

By the same token, you can write to people who are quoted in articles. It's great to see your name in print; in fact there is only one thing better, and that is hearing that someone *else* saw your name in print and now thinks you're a genius. (Of course, you should bear in mind that most of these magazines also carry a help-wanted section.)

These ideas are just some of the many unusual and effective ways to introduce yourself to companies. Browse through all of the sample letters in chapter 7 to uncover other effective ideas.

Mass Mailings and You

Your first effort with a cover letter is to find an individual to whom you can address it. As noted earlier, "Sir/Madam," or "To whom it may concern" says you don't care enough about the company to find out a name—they will pay more attention to the candidates who do. A name shows you have focus and guarantees that a specific individual will open and read your missive. You also have someone to ask for by name when you do your follow-up—important when you are interview hunting.

Must you send out hundreds or even thousands of letters in the coming weeks? I spoke to a woman on a call-in TV show recently who had "done everything and still not gotten a job." She explained how she had sent out almost 300 letters and still wasn't employed. I asked her several questions that elicited some revealing facts: she had been job hunting for almost two years (that equals two or three letters a week) and there were, conservatively, 3,000 companies she could work for (that equals a single approach with no follow-up to only one in ten potential employers). Two employer contacts a week will not get you back to work—or even on the track. Only if you approach and establish communication with every possible employer and follow up properly will you create the maximum opportunity for yourself.

In the world of headhunters the statistical average is 700 contacts between offers and acceptances. These are averages of professionals representing only the most desirable jobs and job candidates to each other. When I hear the oft-quoted statements that it takes a white collar worker about eight months to get a job nowadays, I have a feeling those 700 or so contacts are being spread out needlessly. If you approach the job hunt in a professional manner, the way executive search professionals and employment agents approach their work, you can be happily installed on the next rung of your career ladder within a few weeks or months.

I am not recommending that you immediately make up a list of 700 companies and mail letters to them today. That isn't the answer. Your campaign needs strategy. While every job-hunting campaign is unique, you will want to maintain a balance between the *number* of letters you send out on a daily and weekly basis and the *kinds* of letters you send out.

The key is to send out a balanced mailing representing all the different types of leads, and to send them out regularly and in a volume that will allow you to make follow-up calls. There are many headhunters who manage their time so well that they average over fifty calls a day, year in and year out. While you may aim at building your call volume up to this number, I recommend that you start out with more modest goals.

To start the campaign:

Source	Number of Letters Per Day
Newspaper ads	10
Networking	10 (5 to friends, 5 to professional colleagues)
Direct research contacts (reference works, magazines, etc.)	10
Headhunters	10

Do You Need to Compose More Than One Letter?

Almost certainly. There is a case for all of us having letters and resumes in more than one format. The key is to do each variation once and do it right; and that, as we have seen, means keeping your work comprehensively backed up on disk. This way, even for future job hunts, the leg work will already be done and you'll be ready regardless of when opportunity or necessity comes knocking.

In fact, you may find it valuable to send upwards of half a dozen contact letters to any given company, to assure that they know you are available. To illustrate, let's say you are a young engineer desirous of gaining employment with Last Chance Electronics. It is well within the bounds of reason that you would mail cover or broadcast letters to any or all of the following people, with each letter addressed by name to minimize its chances of going straight into the trash:

- Company President.
- Vice President of Engineering.
- Chief Engineer.
- Engineering Design Manager.
- Vice President of Human Resources.
- Technical Engineering Recruitment Manager.
- Technical Recruiter.

The Plan

A professionally organized and conducted campaign will proceed on one of two plans of attack.

Approach #1

A carefully targeted rifle approach of a select group of companies. You will have first identified these "super-desirable" places to work as you researched your long list of potential employers. You will continue to add to this primary target list as you unearth fresh opportunities in your day-to-day research efforts.

In this instance you have two choices:

1. Mail to everyone at once, remembering that the letters have to be personalized and followed up appropriately.

2. Start your mailings off with one to a line manager and one to a contact in human resources. Follow up in a few days and repeat the process to other names on your hit list.

Approach #2

A carpet-bombing strategy designed to reach every possible employer on the basis that you won't know what opportunities there are unless you go find out. (Here, too, you must personalize and follow up appropriately.)

Begin the process with a mailing to one or two contacts within the company and then repeat the mailings to other contacts when your initial follow-up calls result in referrals or dead ends. Remember, just because Harry in engineering says there are no openings in the company, that's not necessarily the case; always find out for yourself. Don't rely on hearsay. Even if he doesn't have a need himself, any one contact could well know the person who is just dying to meet you.

Once you have received some responses to your mailings and scheduled some interviews, your emphasis will change. Those contacts and interviews will require follow-up letters and conversation. You will be spending time preparing for interviews.

This is exactly the point where most job hunts stall. We get so excited about the interview activity we convince ourselves that "This will be the offer." The headhunters have a saying,

"The offer that can't fail always will." What typically happens is that the offer doesn't materialize, and we are left sitting with absolutely no interview activity. We let the interview funnel empty itself.

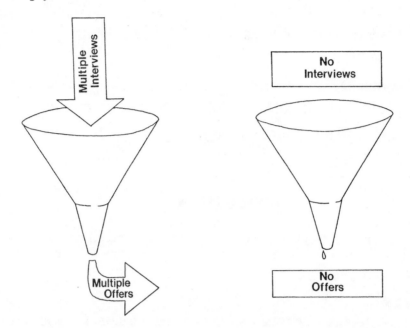

The more letters you send out, the more follow-up calls you can make to schedule interviews. The more interviews you get, the better you feel and the better you get at interviewing. The better you get at interviewing, the more offers you get.

So no matter how good things look, you must continue the campaign—you have to maintain activity with those companies with whom you are in negotiation. But you must also maintain your marketing schedule. The daily plan now looks like this:

```
Source                          Number of Letters Per Day
Newspaper ads                              5
Networking (associations,
   alumni, colleagues)                     5
Direct research contacts
   (reference work,
   magazines, etc.)                        5
Headhunters                                5
Follow-up letters and calls             15-20
```

Small but consistent mailings have many benefits. The balance you maintain is important because most job hunters are tempted simply to send the easy letters and make the easy calls (i.e., network with old friends). Doing this will knock your job hunt out of balance and kick you into a tailspin.

Even when an offer is pending, you must keep plugging, and by that I include all variations on "Harry, you've got the job and we're glad you can start Monday; the offer letter is in the mail." Yeah, just like the check in the proverb. Never accept the "yes" until you have it in writing, have started work, and the first paycheck has cleared at the bank! Until then, keep your momentum building. It is the professional and circumspect thing to do.

Following Up: A Cautionary Tale

In theory, your perfect letter will generate a 100-percent response. But there is no perfect letter and this is a less than perfect world. While you will get calls from your mailing, if you sit there like Buddha waiting for the world to beat a path to your door, you may wait a long time.

Not long ago a pal of mine put a two-line ad in the local paper for a programmer analyst. By Wednesday of the following week he had received over a hundred responses. Ten days later he was still plowing through them when he received a follow-up call (the only one he did receive) from one of the ad respondents. The job hunter was in the office within two hours, returned the following morning, and was hired by lunchtime.

The candidate's paperwork was simply languishing there in the pile waiting to be discovered. The follow-up phone call got it discovered. The call made the interviewer sort through the enormous pile of paper, pull out the letter and resume, and act on it. Follow-up calls work.

You'll notice that many letters in Chapter 7 mention that they will follow up with a phone call. This allows the writer to explain to any inquisitive receptionist that Joe Shmoe is "expecting my call" or that it is "personal."

I find it surprising that so many professionals are nervous about calling a fellow professional on the phone and talking about what they do for a living. After all, isn't this exactly what you do at a party when you run into a fellow professional and stand around talking shop? To help reduce any nervousness, understand that there is an unwritten professional credo shared by the vast majority of successful professional people: You should always help another if it isn't going to hurt you in the process.

If you are not already successful in management, you need to know the principle outlined in my management books *Hiring the Best* and *Keeping the Best*: "The first tenet of management is getting work done through others." It is truly on this single idea that a manager's success rests. Managers are always on the lookout for competent professionals in their field for today and tomorrow. In fact, the best managers maintain a private file of great professionals they can't use today but want to keep available. I know of someone who got a job as a result of a letter retained in these files. She got the interview (and the job) from the broadcast letter she'd sent eight years earlier.

No manager will ever take offense at a call from a competent fellow professional. To know exactly how to make the call and what to say, you will want to look at the chapter entitled "Painting the Perfect Picture on the Phone" in *Knock 'em Dead with Great Answers to Tough Interview Questions.*

To insure that you keep track of the letters you have sent and the results of the follow-up phone calls use this Contact Tracker. I suggest you make a couple hundred copies and put them in a three-ringed binder.

CONTACT TRACKER
DATE _____

COMPANY	TEL #	CONTACT NAME	RESULT	F/U DATE	SENT RESUME
1.					
2.					
3.					
4.					
5.					
6.					
7.					
8.					
9.					
10.					
11.					
12.					
13.					
14.					
15.					
16.					
17.					
18.					
19.					
20.					
21.					
22.					
23.					
24.					
25.					

How to Use the Contact Tracker

Before making a day's mailing, fill out the Contact Tracker with the company name, telephone number, and contact name. This will help you structure your job hunting days. A mailing today will allow you to have a follow-up plan set and ready to go at the appropriate time. As a rule of thumb, a mailing sent today is ripe for follow-up 4 to 8 days from now. Any sooner and you can't be sure the mail has arrived; much later and it may already have gotten lost or been passed on.

You will know that your job hunt is on track when you are filling one Contact Tracker out every day as a result of a mailing, and filling a second one out as a result of your follow-up calls.

If you follow the advice in this book, you will get interviews. If you follow the advice in *Resumes that Knock 'em Dead* and *Knock 'em Dead with Great Answers to Tough Interview Questions*, you will get multiple job offers. When you get your first job offer, you will want to read the section on multiple offers in *Knock 'em Dead with Great Answers to Tough Interview Questions*, which will show you how to turn many of these generated contacts into additional interviews and competitive offers.

Every month I hear from people who use these techniques effectively. Recently I spoke to a gentleman on a radio call-in show who had been out of work for some months. He had bought the books and followed my advice to the letter and had generated four job offers in only five weeks. I have lost count of the number of similar encounters I've had over the years. Follow my advice in letter and spirit and the same good fortune can be yours. After all, good fortune is really only the intersection of opportunity, preparation, and effort.

CHAPTER SEVEN:

SAMPLE LETTERS

NOW WE COME TO THE LETTERS. Apart from the sender's name and address (the personal stationery aspect), all letters adhere to Houghton Mifflin's *Writer's Guide* specifications. To those who might notice these things, it is important we present an impeccable attention to detail.

Response to Newspaper Advertisement

JANE SWIFT

18 Central Park Street   ◆   Anytown, NY 14788
(516) 555-1212

(Date)

Phillip _____
(Title)
ABC Corporation
1 Industry Plaza
Anytown, NY 12096

Dear Mr. _____:

I would like to apply for the programmer position advertised in tomorrow's <u>Sunday Times</u>. Enclosed is my resume.

According to the ad

You want	**I've got**
Three years exp. in Unix C	Four years Unix C experience.
VAX VMS experience	Two years experience total, on a project involving a VAX 11/785 (VAX/VMS).

As I will be traveling from California to New Jersey during the coming week, a message can be left for me at (714) 555-1212.

I look forward to hearing from you. Thank you for your consideration.

Sincerely,

Jane Swift

Jane Swift

JS
enclosure

Response to Newspaper Advertisement

Jane Swift
18 Central Park Street, Anytown, NY 14788
(516) 555-1212

(Date)

Emily _____
(Title)
ABC Corporation
1 Industry Plaza
Anytown, NY 12096

Dear Ms. _____:

I'm writing in response to your ad in *The Sunday* _____ for an editor.

I have a bachelor's degree in communications from _____ University with an advertising major and art minor. My experience includes work at: _____ advertising in Los Angeles, _____ in Portland, as well as freelance writing assignments for the _____ *Journal* and _____ Community College. I've enclosed a few writing samples for your review.

I have extensive editorial, proofreading, layout, and design experience, having served as the editor of my high school yearbook and previously as a section editor and staff member. The yearbook won first place in the _____ High School Press Conference for 19—. Most recently I completed a 32-page catalog paste-up and layout project for _____ Lab sales in Hillsboro.

As a temporary secretary/word-processor I am responsible for creating a wide variety of documents and take great pleasure making sure each document looks good, reads well, and is error-free.

I'm organized and detail-oriented, work well under pressure and on deadline, enjoy working with a variety of people, and have a great attitude. I'm looking for a creative, challenging, growth-oriented position and would like the opportunity to learn more about your company and the position. What you need and what I can do sound like a match! I look forward to hearing from you.

Sincerely yours,

Jane Swift

Jane Swift

JS
enclosures

P.S. I will be out of town until Tuesday, June —th. However, a message may be left at my home number, 555-1212.

Response to Newspaper Advertisement

JAMES SHARPE

18 Central Park Street, Anytown, NY 14788
(516) 555-1212

(Date)

Phillip _____
(Title)
ABC Corporation
1 Industry Plaza
Anytown, NY 12096

Dear Mr. _____ :

Re: File No. 213

I have nine years of accounting experience and am responding to
your recent advertisement for an Accounting Manager. Please allow
me to highlight my skills as they relate to your stated
requirements.

Your Requirements	**My Experience**
A recognized accounting degree plus several years of practical accounting experience.	Obtained a C.A. degree in 1982 and have over four years practical experience as an Accounting Manager.
Excellent people skills and demonstrated ability to motivate staff.	Effectively managed a staff of 24 including two supervisors.
Strong administrative and analytical skills.	Assisted in the development of a base reference library with Lotus 1-2-3 for 400 clients.
Good oral and written communication skills.	Trained four new supervisors via daily coaching sessions, communication meetings, and technical skill sessions.

I believe this background provides the management skills which
you require for this position. I would welcome the opportunity
for a personal interview to further discuss my qualifications.

Yours truly,

James Sharpe

James Sharpe

JS
enclosure

Response to Newspaper Advertisement

JANE SWIFT
18 CENTRAL PARK STREET, ANYTOWN, NY 14788, (516) 555-1212

(Date)

Emily _____
(Title)
ABC Corporation
1 Industry Plaza
Anytown, NY 12096

Dear Ms. _____ :

Please accept this letter as application for the Technical Sales Representative position currently available with your company, as advertised in Sunday's _____ *Globe*. My confidential resume is enclosed for your review and consideration, and I believe you will find me well qualified.

Detailed on my resume you will find a solid background in Sales and Marketing, with over two years in technical sales. In this capacity, I have developed an expertise in new and key account acquisition, new territory development and management, contract negotiation, and customer service. I am confident that my experience in these areas will prove to be an asset to ABC Corporation.

Additionally, I am familiar with blueprints, part number breakdowns, and the bidding process of our major accounts, which include _____, _____, _____ and _____ Corp. I have doubled my sales from $40,000/month to $80,000/month in just two years, and I am known for effectively identifying and resolving problems before they impact related areas, personnel or customers.

I would welcome the opportunity to discuss with you how I might make similar contributions to the success of ABC Corporation. I look forward to hearing from you to schedule a personal interview at your convenience.

Sincere regards,

Jane Swift

Jane Swift

JS
enclosure

Response to Newspaper Advertisement

JANE SWIFT
_____

18 Central Park Street, Anytown, NY 14788 ▪ (516) 555-1212

(Date)

Phillip _____
(Title)
ABC Corporation
1 Industry Plaza
Anytown, NY 12096

Dear Mr. _____:

Re: International Sales Manager, *Globe & Mail*, September —, 19—

I was recently speaking with Mr. _____ from your firm and he strongly recommended that I send you a copy of my resume. Knowing the requirements for the position, he felt that I would be an ideal candidate. For more than eleven years, I have been involved in international sales management, with seven years directly in the aerospace industry. My qualifications for the position include:

- establishing sales offices in France, Great Britain and Germany;
- recruiting and managing a group of 24 international sales representatives;
- providing training programs for all of the European staff which included full briefing on our own products as well as competitor lines;
- obtaining 42%, 33% and 31% of the French, German and British markets, respectively, dealing with all local engine and airframe manufacturers; and
- generating more than $32 million in sales with excellent margins.

My Bachelor of Science degree in electrical engineering was obtained from the University of _____ and my languages include French and German.

I feel confident that an interview would demonstrate that my expertise in setting up rep organizations and training and managing an international sales department would be an excellent addition to your growing aerospace company.

I look forward to meeting with you, Mr. _____, and will give you a call to follow up on this letter the week of (date).

Yours truly,

Jane Swift

Jane Swift

JS
enclosure

Response to Newspaper Advertisement

JAMES SHARPE   8 Central Park Street, Anytown, NY 14788
(516) 555-1212

(Date)

Emily _____
(Title)
ABC Corporation
1 Industry Plaza
Anytown, NY 12096

Dear Ms. _____:

Please accept this letter as application for the Cost Accounting
Supervisor position currently available with your company, as
advertised in the _____ *Telegram* (Sunday, November —th). My
resume is enclosed for review and consideration.

I offer a solid financial background and education, as well as
extensive practical experience in financial applications of
automated systems and Lotus software. My experience includes
monthly financial analysis/reporting and interface with
accounting and administrative management. Additionally, I am
experienced in upgrading and maintaining an ADP D2000
microcomputer system. I am confident that with my abilities I can
make an immediate and valuable contribution to ABC Company.

I look forward to hearing from you in the near future to schedule
an interview at your convenience. I hope to learn more about your
company's plans and goals and how I might contribute to its
continued success.

Best regards,

James Sharpe

James Sharpe

JS
enclosure

Response to Newspaper Advertisement

Jane Swift

18 Central Park Street, Anytown, NY 14788 ▪ (516) 555-1212

(Date)

Phillip _____
(Title)
ABC Corporation
1 Industry Plaza
Anytown, NY 12096

Dear Mr. _____:

In response to your advertisement which appeared in the _____ *Times*, I have enclosed my resume for your consideration.

My experience as an administrative investment banker and assistant to a Vice Chairman is, I believe, readily adaptable to your needs. I have spent five years in a position best described as "doing whatever needs to be done" and have capitalized on my ability to undertake a large and widely varied array of projects, learn quickly, find effective solutions to problems, and maintain a sense of humor throughout.

My years as a line and administrative professional have also provided me with an unusual sensitivity to the needs of senior professionals. I have substantial computer experience and am fully computer literate. I have been told my verbal and written communication skills are exceptional.

I believe your firm would provide a working atmosphere to which I would be well suited, as well as one where my diverse experience would be valuable.

My salary requirements are reasonable and negotiable based on the responsibilities and opportunities presented.

Sincerely,

Jane Swift

Jane Swift

JS
enclosure

Response to Newspaper Advertisement

JANE SWIFT

18 Central Park Street, Anytown, NY 14788 ▪ (516) 555-1212

(Date)

Emily _____
(Title)
ABC Corporation
1 Industry Plaza
Anytown, NY 12096

RE: #4314 Position

Dear Ms. _____:

I am responding to your advertisement in *The Sunday* _____, February —th, for a legal administrator of a law firm. I wrote to you on (date) about law administrator positions in the metropolitan _____ area. I have enclosed another resume of my educational background and employment history. I am very interested in this position.

I have been a legal administrator for two 21-attorney law firms during the past six years. In addition, I have been a law firm consultant for over a year. Besides my law firm experience, I have been a medical administrator for over ten years. I believe that all of this experience will enable me to manage the law firm for this position very successfully. I possess the management, marketing, computer, accounting/budgeting, financial planning, personnel, and people-oriented skills that will have a very positive impact on this law firm.

I will be in the _____ area later in the month, so hopefully, we can meet at that time to discuss this position. I look forward to hearing from you, Ms. _____, concerning this position. Thank you for your time and consideration.

Very truly yours,

Jane Swift

Jane Swift

JS
enclosure

Response to Newspaper Advertisement

JAMES SHARPE

18 Central Park Street ◆ Anytown, NY 14788
(516) 555-1212

(Date)

Box 9412
New York, NY 01234

Dear _____:

I was very pleased to learn of the need for an Executive Assistant in your company from your recent advertisement in _____. I believe the qualities you seek are well matched by my track record:

Your Needs	My Qualifications
Independent Self-Starter	• Served as company liaison between sales representatives, controlling commissions and products. • Controlled cash flow, budget planning and bank reconciliation for three companies. • Assisted in the promotion of a restaurant within a private placement sales effort, creating sales materials and communicating with investors.
Computer Experience	• Utilized Lotus in preparing financial spread sheet used in private placement memorandums and Macintosh to design brochures and flyers. • Have vast experience with both computer programming and the current software packages.
Compatible Background	• Spent 5 years overseas and speak French. • Served as an executive assistant to four corporate heads.

A resume is enclosed that covers my experience and qualifications in greater detail. I would appreciate the opportunity to discuss my credentials in a personal interview.

Sincerely,

James Sharpe

James Sharpe

JS
enclosure

Response to Newspaper Advertisement

Jane Swift
18 Central Park Street, Anytown, NY 14788
(516) 555-1212

(Date)

Human Resources Office (A-570)
_____ Educational Foundation
51 Clark Avenue
Boston, MA 01234

Dear _____:

I've been a member of the _____ Educational Foundation for several years, and rely on you for exceptional programs. I've enclosed my resume and would like to be considered for the position advertised in last Sunday's <u>Globe</u> as Customer Service Supervisor.

I have ten years of business experience, including managerial and supervisory work, and have hired, trained, and supervised high-quality, responsive work groups. In addition to the work you see listed, I've been called upon to help design and facilitate "Face to the Customer" training programs for front-line workers. I also have access television experience, and am, as I said before, quite familar with your programs.

On those occasions when I've spoken to members of your Customer Service staff, they have been very helpful. I'd like a chance to be part of that group and of the _____ Educational Foundation.

I look forward to hearing from you.

Sincerely,

Jane Swift

Jane Swift

JS
enclosure

Response to Newspaper Advertisement (Summer Job)

James Sharpe

---

18 Central Park Street ◆ Anytown, NY 14788
(516) 555-1212

(Date)

Phillip _____
(Title)
ABC Corporation
1 Industry Plaza
Anytown, NY 12096

Dear Mr. _____:

I am excited about your advertisement for a summer intern. An internship with ABC Corporation is an ideal opportunity for me to enhance the skills I am developing as a third year student, majoring in _____ at the University of _____.

The professional competency I have developed in other jobs (see enclosed resume) will enable me to assist you in meeting departmental goals. I would benefit from the experience of working with professionals and for a company with the strongest reputation in the industry.

I would like very much to be part of your team. I am available to meet with you at your convenience.

Sincerely,

James Sharpe

James Sharpe

JS
enclosure

Response to Newspaper Advertisement

JAMES SHARPE
18 Central Park Street, Anytown, NY 14788
(516) 555-1212

(Date)

Emily _____
(Title)
ABC Corporation
1 Industry Plaza
Anytown, NY 12096

Dear Ms. _____:

In response to your _____ ad, please consider my resume in your search for a
Production Supervisor.

With a hi-tech background in Fortune 50 companies, I feel well qualified for the position
you described. I am presently responsible for the coordination of production in three
assembly and test areas which employ 35 union personnel. Maintaining control of work of
this magnitude and complexity requires my ability to function independently, and a
willingness to make decisions quickly and effectively.

I am accustomed to a fast-paced environment where deadlines are priority and handling
multiple jobs simultaneously is the norm. I enjoy a challenge and work hard to attain my
goals. Constant negotiations with all levels of management and union employees have
strengthened my interpersonal skills. I would like very much to discuss with you how I
could contribute to your organization.

I am seeking an opportunity to excel in a more dynamic company and am looking forward
to relocating to the _____ area.

Please contact me at your earliest convenience so that I may share with you my
background and enthusiasm for the job. Thank you for your time and consideration.

Sincerely,

James Sharpe

James Sharpe

JS
enclosure

Response to Newspaper Advertisement

JAMES SHARPE

18 Central Park Street, Anytown, NY 14788
(516) 555-1212

(Date)

Emily _____
(Title)
ABC Corporation
1 Industry Plaza
Anytown, NY 12096

Dear Ms. _____:

Re: Your Ad "Maneater"

There's a tiger in your sights! If you are
prepared to offer this man-eater something to
sink his teeth into, you'll have bagged a
worthy trophy.

In suitable environs, this hunter of
achievement will proudly perform with all the
skill, talent, tenacity and drive at his
command. A resume is enclosed for your perusal.
I will call to talk further.

Very truly yours,

James Sharpe

James Sharpe

JS
enclosure

Response to Newspaper Advertisement

JAMES SHARPE

18 Central Park Street, Anytown, NY 14788
(516) 555-1212

(Date)

Emily _____
(Title)
ABC Corporation
1 Industry Plaza
Anytown, NY 12096

Dear Ms. _____:

I have enclosed a copy of my resume in response to your advertisement in the _____
Journal for a Controller. I have recently sold a business and I am presently looking for a
career opportunity with a progressive company. I offer a high energy level, seasoned
experience and flexible salary requirements.

Respectfully yours,

James Sharpe

James Sharpe

JS
enclosure

POWER PHRASES

Consider using adaptations of these key phrases in your letters responding to advertisements.

I believe that I am particularly well qualified for your position and would like to have the opportunity to meet with you to explore how I may be of value to your organization.

Your advertisement #5188 in the March 25th edition of The _____ has piqued my interest. This position has strong appeal to me.

I am confident that with my abilities I can make an immediate and valuable contribution to _____.

I would be pleased if you contacted me for an interview.

I was recently speaking with Mr. _____ from your firm and he strongly recommended that I send you a copy of my resume. Knowing the requirements for the position, he felt that I would be an ideal candidate.

I feel confident that an interview would demonstrate that my expertise in setting up rep organizations, and training and managing an international sales department would be an excellent addition to your growing _____ company.

I look forward to meeting with you, Mr. _____, and will give you a call to follow up on this letter the week of September —th.

The opportunity to work with your client is appealing to me and I would appreciate an opportunity to discuss the position further. I look forward to hearing from you soon.

I believe this background provides the management skills which you require for this position. I would welcome the opportunity for a personal interview to further discuss my qualifications.

In response to your ad, please consider my resume in your search for a Sales Service Coordinator.

I look forward to hearing from you in the near future to schedule an interview at your convenience, during which I hope to learn more about your company's plans and goals and how I might contribute to the success of its service team.

I am accustomed to a fast-paced environment where deadlines are priority and handling multiple jobs simultaneously is the norm. I enjoy a challenge and work hard to attain my goals. Constant negotiations with all levels of management and union employees have strengthened my interpersonal skills. I would like very much to discuss with you how I could contribute to your organization.

I am seeking an opportunity to excel in a dynamic company and am looking forward to relocating to _____.

Please contact me at your earliest convenience so that I may share with you my background and enthusiasm for the job.

Your ad captured my attention.

My personal goal is simple: I wish to be a part of an organization that wants to excel in both _____ and _____. I believe that if I had the opportunity to interview with you it would be apparent that my skills are far reaching.

Although I'm far more interested in a fine company and an intriguing challenge than merely in money, you should know that in recent years my compensation has been in the range of $35,000 to $50,000.

May we set up a time to talk?

What you need and what I can do sound like a match!

Please find enclosed a copy of my resume for your review. I believe the combination of my _____ education and my business experience offer me the unique opportunity to make a positive contribution to your firm.

I am available to meet with you to discuss my qualifications at your convenience. I can be reached at _____. I would like to thank you in advance for your time and any consideration you may give me. I look forward to hearing from you.

Having been born and raised in the _____ area and wishing to return to this area to work as a _____, I have been researching _____ firms that offer the type of experience for which my previous education and work experience will be of mutual benefit. Highlights of my attached resume include: _____.

Please consider my qualifications for the position of _____ which you advertised.

As you will note on the enclosed resume, the breadth of my expertise covers a wide area of responsibilities, thereby providing me with insights into the total operation.

Recently, I saw an advertisement in the _____ for a position as a Word Processing Trainer. My candidacy for this position is advanced by my experience in three areas: training, support, and a technological background.

I thrive on challenge and feel that my skills and experience are easily transferrable.

I would appreciate an opportunity to discuss my abilities in more depth, and am available for an interview at your earliest convenience.

Is the ideal candidate for the position of _____ highly motivated, professional, and knowledgeable in all functions concerning _____? Well, you may be interested to know that a person possessing these qualities, and much more, is responding to your ad in the _____ for this position.

I very much enjoy working in a team environment and the rewards associated with group contribution.

The skills you require seem to match my professional strengths.

I have a strong background in telemarketing small and medium-size businesses in the _____ District and outlying areas.

I look forward to hearing from you soon to set up an appointment at your convenience. Please feel free to give me a call at my office at _____ or leave a message at my home number, _____.

As a recent MBA graduate, my professional job experience is necessarily limited. However, I believe that you will find, and previous employers will verify, that I exhibit intelligence, common sense, initiative, maturity, stability, and that I am eager to make a positive contribution to your organization.

I read, with a great deal of interest, your advertisement in the October 20 _____.

Please allow me to highlight some of my achievements which relate to your requirements: _____.

I would greatly appreciate the opportunity to discuss this position in a personal interview. I may be contacted at _____ to arrange a meeting.

I would appreciate an opportunity to meet with you. At present I am working as a temp but am available to meet with you at your convenience. I look forward to meeting you.

Thank you for taking the time recently to respond to my questions concerning a _____ position with _____.

I will be in your area Friday, December —th, and will call you early next week to see if we might schedule a meeting at that time.

This experience has provided me with a keen appreciation for the general practice of _____.

A salary of $24,000 would be acceptable, however, my main concern is to find employment where there is potential for growth.

"Cold" Cover Letter—To A Potential Employer

JANE SWIFT

18 Central Park Street ◆ Anytown, NY 14788
(516) 555-1212

(Date)

Phillip _____
(Title)
ABC Corporation
1 Industry Plaza
Anytown, NY 12096

Dear Mr. _____:

Are you looking for a seasoned administrator with diversified experience in human resource management, financial services management, project leadership and operational audits? I have seventeen years of human resources experience with extensive knowledge in staffing, strategic planning, compensation and benefits administration, research and policy development, employee relations and employee relocation.

I am seeking a position in the human resources area; however, I am interested in other administrative management opportunities that require my abilities.

I have enclosed my resume and I look forward to hearing from you to discuss my qualifications further.

Sincerely,

Jane Swift

Jane Swift

JS
enclosure

"Cold" Cover Letter—To A Potential Employer (Summer Job)

JAMES SHARPE   8 Central Park Street, Anytown, NY 14788
                                               (516) 555-1212

(Date)

Emily _____
(Title)
ABC Corporation
1 Industry Plaza
Anytown, NY 12096

Dear Ms. _____:

Your listing in the <u>National Job Bank</u> indicates that you may need
a _____ for a summer internship position. Last summer I
worked for one of your competitors (see attached resume). This
year I intend to build on that foundation with hands-on
experience in _____. As my resume indicates, my education
and other career-oriented work demonstrates that I am a young
professional with a clear focus on my goal of working in the
_____ field. The opportunity to work with a company of your
stature in the industry is my serious intent for the coming year.

Careful planning is a requirement for success in my chosen field.
This is why I am contacting you on my winter break about summer
opportunitites at _____. I will call you to talk further.
Thank you.

Sincerely,

James Sharpe

James Sharpe

JS
enclosure

"Cold" Cover Letter—To A Potential Employer

JAMES SHARPE

18 Central Park Street ◆ Anytown, NY 14788
(516) 555-1212

(Date)

Phillip _____
(Title)
ABC Corporation
1 Industry Plaza
Anytown, NY 12096

Dear Mr. _____:

Please include my name in your job search data base. As requested, I have enclosed a copy of my current resume.

Banking today is definitely a sales environment. While my marketing skills will always be useful, my interests lead me now to seek a more distinct financial management position such as Controller, Treasurer, or Vice President Finance.

Since my CPA will be completed in January 19—, my search may be somewhat premature, but the enclosed transcript and results, combined with my practical experience, should offset my temporary lack of an accounting designation. I would therefore like you to begin considering me immediately. As an Account Manager, I saw many different industries, and so would not feel constrained to any one sector.

Including a mortgage loan benefit, I am currently earning $4,500 per month plus a car allowance. This should provide you with an indication of my present job level. Your suggestions or comments would be appreciated. I am available for interviews, and can be reached at (516) 555-1212. Thank you.

Yours truly,

James Sharpe

James Sharpe

JS
enclosure

"Cold" Cover Letter—To A Potential Employer

JANE SWIFT
18 CENTRAL PARK STREET, ANYTOWN, NY 14788, (516) 555-1212

(Date)

Emily _____
(Title)
ABC Corporation
1 Industry Plaza
Anytown, NY 12096

Dear Ms. _____:

Are you tired of hoping to find something different in an employee? Someone who is more concerned in what she can do for the company, than what the company can do for her? Someone who is self-motivated, instead of someone who waits for you to motivate her? A person who will work for you instead of putting in time?

Well, here I am, striving to meet and surpass your challenges. I feel I can be a great asset to your team, and be a great factor in surpassing your company's goals.

If I seem to represent something different in an employee, try me. I am available for interviews at your convenience.

Thank you for your time!

Sincerely,

Jane Swift

Jane Swift

JS
enclosure

"Cold" Cover Letter—To A Potential Employer

James Sharpe

18 Central Park Street   ◆   Anytown, NY 14788
(516) 555-1212

(Date)

Phillip _____
(Title)
ABC Corporation
1 Industry Plaza
Anytown, NY 12096

Dear Mr. _____:

After fifteen years in the retail administration field, I am seeking a new position and am forwarding my resume for your consideration.

You will notice one common thread throughout my career—I am an administrator and a problem solver. These talents have been applied successfully in office management, field operations, purchasing, communications, telephone skills, organizing and structuring of various departments. These assignments have required close coordination with Senior Management. This diversity of my accomplishments enables me to relate to other areas of business.

I am self-motivated and can work independently to get the job done efficiently in the least possible time.

I will be calling you on Friday, August —th to be sure you received my resume and answer any questions you might have.

Very truly yours,

James Sharpe

James Sharpe

JS
enclosure

"Cold" Cover Letter—To A Potential Employer

JAMES SHARPE
18 Central Park Street, Anytown, NY 14788
(516) 555-1212

(Date)

Alice _____
(Title)
Krieger, Skvetney, Howell
Executive Search Consultants
2426 Foundation Road
Anytown, NY 14788

Dear Ms. _____:

Having spent several years as an executive recruiter, I realize
the number of resumes you receive on a daily basis. However, I
remember how valuable a few always turned out to be.

The purpose of this communication is to introduce myself and then
to meet with you about joining your organization.

In reviewing which business situations have been the most
challenging and rewarding the answer is the time spent in the
search profession.

My background, skills and talents are in all aspects of sales and
sales management. My research indicates that your expertise is in
this area.

I have enclosed a resume which will highlight and support my
objectives. I would appreciate the opportunity to meet and
exchange ideas. I will call you over the next several days to
make an appointment. If you prefer, you may reach me in the
evening or leave a message at (516) 555-1212.

Thank you and I look forward to our meeting.

Sincerely,

James Sharpe

James Sharpe

JS
enclosure

"Cold" Cover Letter—To A Potential Employer

JANE SWIFT

18 Central Park Street, Anytown, NY 14788
(516) 555-1212

(Date)

Emily _____
(Title)
ABC Corporation
1 Industry Plaza
Anytown, NY 12096

Dear Ms. _____ :

Perhaps you are seeking an addition to your communications team. A new person can provide innovative approaches to the challenges and opportunities of integrated corporate communications. You will discover from the enclosed resume that I have a results-oriented background in several key areas.

Although my career has centered around well established public relations agencies, I prefer to continue professionally on the client side. In fact, in a couple of instances (in the United States and overseas), I worked on site within the client organizations.

I want to concentrate my diverse talents in the service of one company's communications efforts. I currently would consider opportunities in the $65-85K range.

Feel free to call me to discuss any details.

Regards,

Jane Swift

Jane Swift

JS
enclosure

"Cold" Cover Letter—To A Potential Employer

JAMES SHARPE

18 Central Park Street, Anytown, NY 14788
(516) 555-1212

(Date)

Phillip _____
(Title)
ABC Corporation
1 Industry Plaza
Anytown, NY 12096

Dear Mr. _____:

Please accept this letter as application for the Process Engineer position currently available with your company. My confidential resume is enclosed for your review and consideration.

My experience has afforded me exposure to numerous facets of process engineering, including troubleshooting, problem solving, tooling set-up, performance improvement projects, and quality assurance. I am confident that my expertise in these areas will prove to be an asset to ABC Company's manufacturing operations.

My current salary requirement would range mid to high-20K's, with specifics flexible, negotiable, and dependent upon such factors as benefit structure, responsibility, and advancement opportunity.

I look forward to hearing from you in the near future to schedule an interview at your convenience, during which I hope to learn more about your company, its plans and goals, and how I might contribute to its continued success.

Sincerely,

James Sharpe

James Sharpe

JS
enclosure

"Cold" Cover Letter—To A Potential Employer (Summer Job)

James Sharpe

18 Central Park Street, Anytown, NY 14788 ▪ (516) 555-1212

(Date)

Emily _____
(Title)
ABC Corporation
1 Industry Plaza
Anytown, NY 12096

Dear Ms. _____:

    I am currently a senior in high school and looking forward
to gaining some real-world professional experience this summer.
My enclosed resume shows that I have had one and a half years
experience as head lifeguard at the _____ Yacht Club.

    This work has helped me develop the necessary people skills
to deal effectively and diplomatically with children of all ages
and their parents. I have experience in shift scheduling, and
understand first-hand the problems employers experience with
younger workers.

    I am able, willing and manageable. I am eager to gain summer
employment related to my ongoing educational and career goals of
a career and degree in physical education.

Yours truly,

James Sharpe

James Sharpe

JS
enclosure

P.S. I am certified in all state first aid requirements and am
also certified in CPR.

"Cold" Cover Letter—To A Potential Employer

JANE SWIFT

18 Central Park Street ◆ Anytown, NY 14788
(516) 555-1212

(Date)

Phillip _____
(Title)
ABC Corporation
1 Industry Plaza
Anytown, NY 12096

Dear Mr. _____:

Re: Executive Assistant Position

Your time is valuable; so is mine. I'm interested in the above opening. My hat is thrown into the ring!

Sincerely,

Jane Swift

Jane Swift

JS
enclosure

"Cold" Cover Letter—To A Potential Employer

JANE SWIFT

18 Central Park Street, Anytown, NY 14788
(516) 555-1212

(Date)

Emily _____
(Title)
ABC Corporation
1 Industry Plaza
Anytown, NY 12096

Dear Ms. _____:

I am very interested in obtaining a position with your organization. Enclosed please find my resume for your review.

You will find most of the necessary background information contained in my resume. However, I would like to mention that I am available for immediate employment. I am also exploring the job market to obtain a position with a firm that will appreciate my skills and willingness to work eagerly with other people. I can definitely offer you longevity.

As my resume indicates, I am a filipina and only arrived in the United States in 19— after my marriage to an American. I hope that this will explain my limited work record in this country. Also, English is the second language in the Philippines. It is spoken from childhood and is taught from grade one in school, so that I am fluent in the language. Frankly, all I need to prove my abilities is an employer who is looking for an employee that is used to hard work with a strong work ethic.

I would like very much to schedule a personal interview wherein we can discuss both my enthusiasm and qualifications for a position with your organization. I can be reached at the address and telephone number listed above.

Thank you for your time; I look forward to a favorable response.

Sincerely yours,

Jane Swift

Jane Swift

JS
enclosure

"Cold" Cover Letter—To A Potential Employer

JANE SWIFT

18 Central Park Street, Anytown, NY 14788
(516) 555-1212

(Date)

Phillip _____
(Title)
ABC Corporation
1 Industry Plaza
Anytown, NY 12096

Dear Mr. _____ :

I received your name from Mr. _____ last week. I spoke to him regarding career opportunities with _____ and he suggested contacting you. He assured me that he would pass my resume along to you; however, in the event that he did not, I am enclosing another.

As an avid cosmetics consumer, I understand and appreciate the high standards of quality that your firm honors. As you can see from my enclosed resume, I have had quite a bit of experience in the international arena. My past experience working overseas has brought me a greater understanding of international cultures and traditions as well as a better understanding and appreciation of our own culture. These insights would certainly benefit a corporation, such as your own, with worldwide locations. In addition, I have gained first hand experience in the consumer marketplace through my various sales positions. I have noticed your recent expansion into the television media and am sure that an energetic individual would surely be an asset to ABC in this, as well as other, projects.

I would very much like to discuss career opportunities with ABC. I will be calling you within the next few days to set up an interview. In the meantime, if you have any questions I may be reached at the number above. Thank you for your consideration.

Sincerely,

Jane Swift

Jane Swift

JS
enclosure

POWER PHRASES

Consider using adaptations of these key phrases in your "cold" letters to potential employers.

My twenty-two-year operations management career with a multi-billion dollar _____ company has been at increasing degrees of responsibility. While I have spent the last five years in top management, I am especially proud of my record—I started as a driver many years ago, and like cream, have risen to the top. I have consistently accomplished all goals assigned to me, particularly overall cost reductions, improved productivity, and customer service. Some of my achievements are:

Your recent acquisition of the _____ chain would indicate an intent to pursue southeastern market opportunities more vigorously than you have in the past several years. I believe that my retail management background would complement your long-range strategy for _____ very effectively.

With the scarcity of qualified technical personnel that exists today, it is my thought that you would be interested in my qualifications as set forth in the attached resume.

In approximately three months I am moving to _____ with my family, and am bringing with me fifteen solid years of banking experience—the last eight in branch operations management. I would like particularly to utilize this experience with your firm.

I have noticed that you conduct laser exposure testing at your facility. If there is a need for laser technicians in this endeavor, I would like to be considered for a position.

As you can see from my resume, I am a psychology major and was president of our debating society in my senior year. I feel both would indicate a talent for sales. I did some selling in my summer job in 19— (ABC Books), and found not only that I was successful, but that I thoroughly enjoyed it.

The position which you described sounds challenging and interesting. After receiving your comments about the job requirements, I am convinced that I can make an immediate contribution toward the growth of _____ and would certainly hope that we may explore things further at your convenience.

The opportunity to put to use my medical knowledge as well as my English degree would bring me great pleasure, and it would please me to know that I was bringing quality to your company.

I feel that the combination of _____'s educational environment and my desire to learn as much as possible about the data processing field could only bring about positive results.

If you think after talking to me and reading my resume that there might be an interest with your client company, I would be very interested. I have been put in many situations where I had to learn quickly, and have always enjoyed the challenge.

My accomplishments include:

You will notice one common thread throughout my career—I am an administrator and a problem solver.

Currently I would like to consider opportunities in the $65-$85K range.

My confidential resume is enclosed for your review and consideration.

My current salary requirement would range mid to high $20Ks, with specifics flexible, negotiable and dependent upon such factors as benefit structure, responsibility, and advancement opportunity.

Having spent several years as a _____, I realize the number of resumes you receive on a daily basis. However, I remember how valuable a few always turned out to be.

My research indicates that your expertise is in this area.

I would like the opportunity to discuss with you how we could mutually benefit one another. You may leave a message on my answering service at my home and I will return the call. I look forward to hearing from you very soon.

This job does seem to be the right challenge for me; I know that with my strong Cobol skills and manufacturing background experience I will be an asset to your company.

Hoping to meet you in person, I thank you for your time.

I will be calling you on Friday, August —, 19— to be sure you received my resume and to answer any questions you might have.

I have enclosed a resume which will highlight and support my objectives. I would appreciate the opportunity to meet and exchange ideas. I will call you over the next several days to make an appointment. If you prefer, you may reach me in the evening or leave a message at (516) 555-1212.

"Cold" Cover Letter—To Employment Industry Professional

James Sharpe
18 Central Park Street, Anytown, NY 14788
(516) 555-1212

(Date)

Bob _____
(Title)
Krieger, Skvetney, Howell
Executive Search Consultants
2426 Foundation Road
Anytown, NY 14788

Dear Mr. _____:

Last week, thirteen major financial institutions reported depressed earnings due to substantial increases in real estate loan losses. In October of 19—, _____ magazine noted that market leading _____ Bank was "overwhelmed by problem real estate loans."

The depressed real estate market characterizing the southwest is rapidly spreading, causing huge problems for insurance companies and leading banks. Many of these institutions are hiring workout officers experienced in the problems of the _____ market. But your clients need to think a step beyond these problems and address—now, in an effective, decisive plan—how they will respond when they are beseiged by foreclosures. They need to put in place executives who understand real estate and who know how to take decisive action, and not just be caretakers. If they do not take this step, they will repeat the asset draining errors made by the southwest banks.

I've seen these errors first hand. I've watched bewildered bank accountants and asset "managers" drive away rent paying tenants, alienate the brokerage community, and bleed their institutions with operating losses. For a financial institution to survive this overbuilt and recessionary climate, it is going to have to implement a strategy calling for personnel experienced in all aspects of commercial real estate to give it a realistic grasp on asset quality, to optimize asset value, and to maximize cash flow.

My background covers over twelve years experience in all aspects of commercial real estate—property management, development, finance, brokerage and acquisitions. I have taken major projects from conception through completion and have hands-on bottom line experience in management, leasing, and in working with properties in depressed markets.

page 1 of 2

In the October 19— edition of *Forbes*, Forbes Four Hundred member _____ succinctly diagnosed the collapse of so many of today's giant syndicators: "They don't have anybody in there who understands what the product of real estate is." Don't let your clients make the same mistake.

I have enclosed for your review a brief resume which outlines my experience. If I may provide you with additional information, please contact me at _____ or the address given above. I look forward to discussing my qualifications with you in more detail.

Sincerely,

James Sharpe

James Sharpe

JS
enclosure

page 2 of 2

94

"Cold" Cover Letter—To Employment Industry Professional

JANE SWIFT   18 Central Park Street, Anytown, NY 14788
(516) 555-1212

(Date)

Alice _____
(Title)
Krieger, Skvetney, Howell
Executive Search Consultants
2426 Foundation Road
Anytown, NY 14788

Dear Ms. _____:

After more than fifteen years of progressive experience in warehousing, I am seeking a new position where my abilities can be utilized fully.

As you can see from the enclosed resume, I have a record of consistently producing results in managing systems and warehouse areas. I enjoy the challenge of investigating and solving administrative problems.

The position I am looking for should have a salary in the range of $26,000-$40,000. Please let me know if my experience and abilities may be of interest to any of your client companies. I will, of course, be happy to meet with you to discuss further details of my experience.

Sincerely,

Jane Swift

Jane Swift

JS
enclosure

"Cold" Cover Letter—To Employment Industry Professional

JANE SWIFT

18 Central Park Street ◆ Anytown, NY 14788
(516) 555-1212

(Date)

Bob _____
(Title)
Krieger, Skvetney, Howell
Executive Search Consultants
2426 Foundation Road
Anytown, NY 14788

Dear Mr. _____:

In the course of your search assignments, you may have a requirement for an organized and goal-directed Vice President. My present position provides me with the qualifications and experience necessary to successfully fulfill a Vice President position. Key strengths which I possess for the success of an administrative position include:

- Direct line operations responsibility improving gross margin to 8.0%.
- Planning and developing over $15 million in new construction projects
- Reduction of departmental operating expenses to 1.1% below budget.
- Negotiation and developing contractual arrangements with vendors.

I have the ability to define problems, assess both large-scale and smaller implications of a project, and implement solutions.

The enclosed resume briefly outlines my administrative and business background. My geographic preferences are the midwest and southeast regions of the country. Relocating to a client's location does not present a problem. Also, I possess a M.B.A. degree from _____ University, and a B.S. degree in Business Administration from _____University. Depending upon location and other factors, my salary requirements would be between $40,000 and $50,000.

If it appears that my qualifications meet the need of one of your clients, I will be happy to further discuss my background in a meeting with you or in an interview with the client. I will be contacting your office in the near future to determine the status of my application.

Sincerely,

Jane Swift

Jane Swift

JS
enclosure

"Cold" Cover Letter—To Employment Industry Professional

JAMES SHARPE

18 Central Park Street ◆ Anytown, NY 14788
(516) 555-1212

(Date)

Alice _____
(Title)
Krieger, Skvetney, Howell
Executive Search Consultants
2426 Foundation Road
Anytown, NY 14788

Dear Ms. _____:

After a nineteen-year career in customer service and operations
support with a leading data processing service company, I am
seeking a position where my experience and skills can be more
fully realized. Positions which fall within the scope of my goals
and abilities are:

        Manager of Customer Service
        Manager of Quality Assurance/Production Control
        Manager of Mailing/Fulfillment Operations.

My record is one of increased responsibility, variety in job
assignments, and solid accomplishments. My experience and skills
are in problem solving, coordinating resources, data processing
and support activities.

The enclosed resume will provide a more complete summation of my
background. My preference for job site is within the state of
California. My salary requirements is in the $35,000 to $40,000
range.

Please contact me if my qualifications match any current openings
and to discuss my background further.

Sincerely,

James Sharpe

JS
enclosure

"Cold" Cover Letter—To Employment Industry Professional

JAMES SHARPE
18 CENTRAL PARK STREET, ANYTOWN, NY 14788, (516) 555-1212

(Date)

Bob _____
(Title)
Krieger, Skvetney, Howell
Executive Search Consultants
2426 Foundation Road
Anytown, NY 14788

Dear Mr. _____:

The enclosed record of successful sales and sales/management may be of interest to you and your clients.

My experience with route sales and route sales personnel covers a period of eleven years. I have dealt directly with chain buyers, store managers and other sales personnel. I would appreciate it if you would read my resume and advise me of an opportunity to meet with you for an interview.

Thank you for your interest.

Sincerely,

James Sharpe

James Sharpe

JS
enclosure

"Cold" Cover Letter—To Employment Industry Professional

James Sharpe

18 Central Park Street, Anytown, NY 14788 ▪ (516) 555-1212

(Date)

Alice _____
(Title)
Krieger, Skvetney, Howell
Executive Search Consultants
2426 Foundation Road
Anytown, NY 14788

Dear Ms. _____:

In the course of your search assignments, you may have a need for an experienced consumer products sales executive. I have enjoyed a progressive career with ABC Company for the last twelve years.

My background, which is detailed in the enclosed resume, includes:

- Promotions through six professional and sales management positions in twelve years. Strengths in recruiting, training, and organization improvement.
- A unique experience base encompassing both retail and institutional sales management.
- A demonstrated track record in both line and staff assignments.

The company is in the process of restructuring the sales organization, thereby limiting the number of advancement opportunities, so I have made the decision to explore career advancement potential outside of XYZ Company.

My preference is to live in the _____ area, but I'm far more interested in fine company with opportunity and challenge. My total compensation this year will be in the mid-nineties. Enclosed is a resume that summarizes my experience. Should my qualifications appear to match the needs of your clients, I would like to explore the opportunity.

Sincerely.

James Sharpe

James Sharpe

JS
enclosure

99

POWER PHRASES

Consider using adaptations of these key phrases in your "cold" letters to employment service professionals.

I am an optimist, thrive on challenges, lead by example, and readily adapt to situations. If your client—international or domestic—would benefit from these kinds of successes we should get to know each other. If you will call or write at your convenience, I look forward to telling more about my background.

An industry association referred to _____ as an active and selective executive search firm, and mentioned your name because of your work in logistics. I liked that referral and think our meeting would be mutually beneficial.

I would like to talk with you personally to further discuss our meeting. I suggest next week, the week of October —, when you have a free minute. I have asked my staff to forward your message immediately in case I am unavailable when you call. I look forward to hearing from you.

Please include my name in your job search data base.

Including a mortgage loan benefit, I am currently earning $4,500 per month plus a car allowance. This should provide you with an indication of my present job level. Your suggestions or comments would be appreciated.

One of your clients is looking for me, if not today then sometime in the near future. I know good people are hard to find because I've had to find them myself.

I have the depth of experience it takes to make a positive contribution.

Income is in the mid five figures, but the right opportunity is the motivating factor. References and resume are available. With my well rounded professional background I look forward to a new and interesting career opportunity through your firm.

The following are some highlights of my track record for your consideration:

I understand your clients frequently ask you to locate senior operating executives with much higher than average ability to accomplish difficult jobs, quickly and profitably.

Please call at your convenience this week so we can explore potential opportunities more fully. Use the home number, please; our company's uncertain financial status is stirring up the office rumor mill. Thank you for your time and attention.

Broadcast Letter

James Sharpe
18 Central Park Street, Anytown, NY 14788
(516) 555-1212

(Date)

Alice _____
(Title)
Krieger, Skvetney, Howell
Executive Search Consultants
2426 Foundation Road
Anytown, NY 14788

Dear Ms. _____:

I am an experienced information systems executive who can make a major contribution for one of your clients. During my career with blue-chip companies including _____, _____, and _____, I have improved the efficiency of their information processing. These improvements include:

- implementing cost reductions totalling more than $1,000,000,
- recommending and/or implementing organizational changes to streamline the organization yet improve customer service.
- taking a leadership position in the introduction of new methods or technologies.
- automating operations (reduced head count).
- upgrading hardware and software from mainframes to PCs (improved quality, cost effectiveness and service levels), and integrating multiple vendors (IBM, DEC, Honeywell).

With the leading integrated professional services firm in the U.S., I developed a methodology to assess clients' information processing effectivenessee, resulting in prioritized recommendations for improvement and increased linkage to achieving business objectives. This has led to billings in excess of $3 million.

My formal education includes an M.B.A. and a B.S. in Engineering. I am seeking a change of employment that will return me to industry in an information systems executive position. While the majority of my experience has been in manufacturing environments, I have consulted in several others. Potential positions of interest would include Information Systems Director or Manager of Data Processing.

Although negotiable depending upon location and other factors, you should know that in recent years, my compensation has been in the range of $85,000 to $100,000.

I would be happy to discuss my background in a meeting with you. If you have any questions, do not hesitate to contact me at my home, or office at _____.

Sincerely yours,

James Sharpe

James Sharpe

JS

101

Broadcast Letter

JAMES SHARPE
18 CENTRAL PARK STREET, ANYTOWN, NY 14788, (516) 555-1212

(Date)

Phillip _____
(Title)
ABC Corporation
1 Industry Plaza
Anytown, NY 12096

Dear Mr. _____:

As an industrial safety and health officer with experience in a unionized heavy manufacturing environment, I feel my background may be of interest to you. My qualifications include:

- A degree in Industrial Relations and Personnel.
- Five years of experience in planning, developing, implementing and maintaining programs designed to prevent occupational injury, illness and property damage—as well as complementary safety contests, individual recognition programs, and safety promotions.
- Experience in the use of industrial hygiene monitoring equipment such as noise dosimeters, air sampling pumps, detector tubes, toxic and explosive gas monitors, etc., and in field investigation of serious incidents and work refusals.
- Administration of employer correspondence concerning claims tor compensation benefits or company appeals, including communications with injured workers, their representatives, benefits staff, and the company lawyer.

In addition to the above, I have been actively involved with the formulation of accident prevention policies and safety rules and procedures. I have also handled grievances and arbitrations concerning safety issues and abuse of the workers compensation system.

In the event that you feel I might be able to assist your organization's occupational health and safety program, I would welcome the opportunity of a personal interview.

Yours truly,

James Sharpe

James Sharpe

JS

Broadcast Letter

JANE SWIFT
18 Central Park Street, Anytown, NY 14788
(516) 555-1212

                                                    (Date)

Emily _____
(Title)
ABC Corporation
1 Industry Plaza
Anytown, NY 12096

Dear Ms. _____:

You may have need for someone with my programming and analyst
background. Some of my recent accomplishments are:

- Developed VSAM I/O interface program in Assembler using
  Access Method Service Macros.
- Collected data and analyzed most of the Master Record
  Trailer-built modules for the on-line Entry Transaction in
  both Assembler and COBOL.
- Developed and implemented programs to generate Assembler
  macros for update programs.
- Collected information and analyzed, designed, coded and
  tested programs in both Assembler and COBOL. Also wrote
  program specifications.
- Developed CICS on-line data communication programs to
  report on fishing vessel weight, volume and weight of the
  catch, and other identifying information.
- Maintained the Accounts Receivable system, the Personal
  Licensing system, the Catch Statistics System, and the
  Sport Fisherman Logbook system with two to four programmers
  under my supervision.
- Converted Xerox programs to IBM programs in COBOL and
  FORTRAN.

I have a B.Sc. in Computer Science and have taken many additional
technical education courses.

I would be pleased to provide further details of my experience in
a personal meeting.

                              Sincerely,

                              Jane Swift

                              Jane Swift

JS

Broadcast Letter

JAMES SHARPE

18 Central Park Street ◆ Anytown, NY 14788
(516) 555-1212

(Date)

Phillip _____
(Title)
Krieger, Skvetney, Howell
Executive Search Consultants
2426 Foundation Road
Anytown, NY 14788

Dear Mr. _____:

If you are looking for a successful executive to take charge of new product marketing, you will be interested in talking to me.

Ten years of experience in every aspect of marketing and sales in different industries gives me the confidence to be open to opportunities in almost any field. My search is focused on companies that innovate because I am particularly effective at new product marketing. I have successfully managed new product marketing research, launch planning, advertising, product training, and sales support, as well as direct sales. In my current position with XYZ Company, I created several products and marketing approaches on which other operating divisions in the company based their programs.

My business education includes a Marketing MBA from _____ University's School of Management, and provides me with a variety of useful analytical tools in managing problems and maximizing opportunities. My superior sales track record guarantees that I bring the reality of the marketplace to each business situation; I know what sells and why.

Currently, my total compensation package brings me in the low seventies; I am looking for a company that rewards performance consistently.

Since I am currently weighing several interesting opportunities, please contact me immediately if you are conducting any searches which might be a good fit. Relocation is no problem.

Thank you in advance for your consideration.

Sincerely,

James Sharpe

James Sharpe

JS

104

Broadcast Letter

JAMES SHARPE

18 Central Park Street, Anytown, NY 14788 ▪ (516) 555-1212

(Date)

Emily _____
(Title)
ABC Corporation
1 Industry Plaza
Anytown, NY 12096

Dear Ms. _____:

Please accept this letter as application for the _____ position currently available with your company in the _____ area, as advertised in the _____ *Globe* (July —, 19—).

I offer a successful background in sales and marketing as well as an education in the sciences. My experience has afforded me exposure to many aspects of sales including prospecting, account acquisition, territory management and development, and customer service. I have been recognized by my current employer for numerous achievements, and I am confident that I can make similar contributions to ABC Corporation.

My education has given me a broad exposure to science and psychology, knowledge which I am sure will be valuable in this position. Additionally, my father is a physician and I was exposed to medical terminology all my life. I believe that this background and exposure will prove to be an asset in selling your products.

Since beginning with XYZ Company, my average commission has progressed from $400 to $650 weekly. My current salary or commission requirement would range upwards of the mid-twenties, with specifics flexible and negotiable.

I look forward to hearing from you in the near future to schedule an interview at your convenience, during which I hope to learn more about the position, your company's plans and goals, and how I can contribute to the success of your sales team.

Sincere regards,

James Sharpe

James Sharpe

JS

Broadcast Letter

JANE SWIFT

18 Central Park Street, Anytown, NY 14788
(516) 555-1212

(Date)

Bob _____
(Title)
Krieger, Skvetney, Howell
Executive Search Consultants
2426 Foundation Road
Anytown, NY 14788

Dear Mr. _____:

I recently learned of your firm's excellent record of matching senior marketing executives with top corporations. I also have learned that you have an officer-level marketing assignment in process now—I am a serious candidate for your client's vacancy. Please consider some successes:

- After joining _____ as Marketing Director, I revitalized a declining processed meats product category in less than a year, introducing better-tasting formulas and actually reducing product costs by over $100,000. Dramatic new packaging enhanced appetite appeal, and fresh promotion strategies doubled previous sales records.
- I have carefully crafted and fine-tuned many new product introductions and line extensions, such as _____ turkey, _____ processed meats, and _____'s deodorant maxi-pads.
- My sales/marketing experience dates from 1975 when I formed a direct sales company to pay for my _____ MBA (now the top-rated program in the U.S.A., I'm proud to say). Much of my subsequent success springs from strong working relationships with sales management and joint sales calls with field reps and marketing brokers. I have designed events like the _____ program, and _____'s sponsorship of the Indy 500 Williams racing team.
- I have a strong personal and professional interest in consumer electronics. I consult professionally and have successfully adapted marketing techniques for home and commercial satellite systems, "high tech" audio/video, and radio communications equipment.

Please inform your client I am fluent in French and I quickly absorb other languages. If your client challenges executives with the greatest of responsibilities and rewards them for remarkable performance, please contact me as soon as possible. I'll quickly repeat my past successes.

Sincerely,

Jane Swift

Jane Swift

JS

Broadcast Letter

JANE SWIFT

---

18 Central Park Street, Anytown, NY 14788
(516) 555-1212

(Date)

Alice _____
(Title)
Krieger, Skvetney, Howell
Executive Search Consultants
2426 Foundation Road
Anytown, NY 14788

Dear Ms. _____:

    I understand your client wants you to locate a Vice President of Marketing/Sales to create a new and aggressive business development function. I have successfully created and developed three marketing and sales functions. My association with leading companies and my track record of consistent accomplishments and increasing responsibility make me a viable candidate. My expertise will quickly achieve competitive advantage for your client.

    While Vice President of Marketing and Strategic Planning at _____ Utility Services (a subsidiary of _____ Energy specializing in financial services, data and software), I . . .

- Created a high-energy, highly-skilled team of inside technical and sales personnel. This team and our external telemarketing and direct marketing companies increased customers 39% in a low growth industry.
- Grew our basic service 128% and increased revenue another 31%.
- Achieved a remarkable 16% direct response rate from senior financial executives and won a direct marketing award from an industry magazine. Two of our direct mail packages made the national finals for the prestigious direct marketing Echo awards presented by the Direct Marketing Association (DMA).

    While Manager of the International Consulting Division at _____ I assisted in creating and developing this new division. From $0 we developed over $2.3 million in new business in only one year. I developed business worldwide by interacting with foreign nationals (public and private sector).

    My demonstrated skills at quickly increasing new business would be most valued by a leading service firm desiring rapid growth and competitive advantage. Relocation would not be an issue. I look forward to hearing from you. I'll be available in the office this next week.

Sincerely,

Jane Swift

Jane Swift

JS

Broadcast Letter

James Sharpe

18 Central Park Street, Anytown, NY 14788 ■ (516) 555-1212

(Date)

Bob _____
(Title)
Krieger, Skvetney, Howell
Executive Search Consultants
2426 Foundation Road
Anytown, NY 14788

Dear Mr. _____:

One of your clients is looking for me, if not today then sometime
in the near future. I know good people are hard to find because
I've had to find them myself.

In over twenty years of retail and wholesale marketing I have
gained the knowledge and insight necessary to successfully
address the many challenges presented in an ever-changing
marketplace. Whether it is by increasing gross margin, reducing
expenses, boosting sales, or managing a large department, I have
the depth of experience it takes to make a positive contribution.

I am single (43) with no dependents and able to relocate
anywhere. Income is in the mid five figures, but the right
opportunity is the motivating factor. With my well rounded
professional background I look forward to a new and interesting
career opportunity through your firm.

Sincerely,

James Sharpe

James Sharpe

JS

Broadcast Letter

James Sharpe
18 Central Park Street, Anytown, NY 14788
(516) 555-1212

(Date)

Alice _____
(Title)
Krieger, Skvetney, Howell
Executive Search Consultants
2426 Foundation Road
Anytown, NY 14788

Dear Ms. _____:

I have heard that you conduct searches for clients seeking senior executives with proven abilities, strong track records and international experience. I have recently returned to the USA from Argentina and it's unlikely you will find me through your normal sources, so I've decided to write directly and introduce myself.

American businesses starting up in Europe or Latin America will struggle against entrenched foreign competition and huge cultural differences. I've faced these and handled them more successfully than most Americans.

After becoming General Manager of a high quality bakery company in Buenos Aires, Argentina, I reorganized sales, distribution and warehousing. I rebuilt the demoralized sales force with leadership, communication and enthusiasm. I set up an American-style distribution network to supply supermarkets, distributors, and smaller stores in the interior. After only a year, improvements I introduced expanded business 100-fold to two bakeries on 24-hour shifts, with 150 employees and sixteen trucks selling nationally.

With _____ (international public accountants and consultants), I consulted with principals of closely-held Argentinian companies, particularly in general management, distribution, administration, and merchandizing of industrial and consumer products. We quite successfully increased market share, built output, and added new outlets.

Before moving to Argentina, I built and directed a family-owned grocery chain (to eleven supermarkets, 850 employees and $60 million in sales from two stores and only $4.5 million) in a highly competitive Florida market. The company established a reputation for quality perishables and outstanding customer service; we introduced the first 24-hour supermarket in Florida.

page 1 of 2

My wife and I returned to the U.S. because of Argentina's high inflation and an unstable political climate. I am an optimist, thrive on challenges, lead by example and readily adapt to situations. If your client— international or domestic—would benefit from these kinds of successes we should get to know each other. If you will call or write at your convenience, I look forward to telling more about my background.

Sincerely,

James Sharpe

James Sharpe

JS

Broadcast Letter

JAMES SHARPE
18 CENTRAL PARK STREET, ANYTOWN, NY 14788, (516) 555-1212

(Date)

Bob _____
(Title)
Krieger, Skvetney, Howell
Executive Search Consultants
2426 Foundation Road
Anytown, NY 14788

Dear Mr. _____:

An industry association referred to your organization as an active and selective executive search firm, and mentioned your name because of your work in logistics. I liked that referral and think our meeting would be mutually beneficial.

I have a successful career of using logistics to cut costs and improve profits, usually in concert with other parts of the business. For example:

- I supervised the start-up of several remote offices to assist our plants in improving their distribution operations. By offering customized service and through sharp negotiations, we saved over $500 million in various operations and warehouse costs.
- I directed the efforts of sizeable computer resources in the design and installation of a major application that saved $2.5 million in carrier costs. The application became the standard throughout the company's 46 locations.
- Working with International Sales, I have established various Quality Control programs that have improved the timeliness and accuracy of product and paperwork delivery. Customer complaints plummetted to virtually zero, and remain there today.

A recent reorganization has reduced the number of senior management positions available within my company. I have concluded that another firm may offer a position and career advancement more in line with my personal expectations.

I would like to talk with you further. I suggest next week, the week of October 29, when you have a free minute. I have asked my staff to forward your message immediately in case I am unavailable when you call. I look forward to hearing from you.

Sincerely,

James Sharpe

James Sharpe

JS

111

Broadcast Letter

JAMES SHARPE

---

18 Central Park Street, Anytown, NY 14788   ▪   (516) 555-1212

(Date)

Emily _____
(Title)
ABC Corporation
1 Industry Plaza
Anytown, NY 12096

Dear Ms. _____:

NINE REASONS WHY YOU SHOULD HIRE JAMES SHARPE

1. Five years of success in various aspects of the broadcast industry (AM, FM and TV) provides a unique knowledge of the business.
2. Four years of successful selling attests to ability to win consistently.
3. Management training in all departments of radio and television has provided an overall understanding of broadcast operations.
4. Plans the tasks that lead to achievement of sales objectives.
5. Maintains control of several simultaneous activities so they stay on schedule.
6. Is enterprising, resourceful, and results-oriented—a closer!
7. Has ability to solve problems with sound professional judgment and a minimum of supervision.
8. Contributes to the company's profitability while motivating and working effectively with colleagues.
9. Has the personal and professional respect of past and present managers.

Call him at 555-1212.

Sincerely,

James Sharpe

James Sharpe

JS

112

Broadcast Letter

JANE SWIFT

18 Central Park Street, Anytown, NY 14788
(516) 555-1212

(Date)

Bob _____
(Title)
Krieger, Skvetney, Howell
Executive Search Consultants
2426 Foundation Road
Anytown, NY 14788

Dear Mr. _____:

If information just reaching me is timely, this letter isn't too late. I understand your client has asked you to locate a *truly* exceptional VP of _____ with well-developed leadership and (especially) promotional skills. In ten years with _____, I've proven I have these and an unusually strong ability to accomplish difficult service industry financial goals.

- Managers and executives around _____ were scarce; we had to locate and rely on bright, ambitious beginners. I have shown I am much better at developing subordinates than most. My hires have consistently moved up to senior positions in transportation, marketing, and operations.
- _____ was in a difficult position after following five major competitors into a fragmented _____ market. I isolated our best market—low-cost frequent visitors—through intense research.
- The _____ industry often overlooks ancillary business. To improve customer quality and service, I discovered an important cash advance and credit card processing opportunity. By negotiating with new banks, cash advance procedures I instituted produced $2.5 million in profits annually.

I left the _____ Organization as a Senior VP earlier this year to consult, but have concluded my contributions will be much more significant as a team player VP once again. I decided to contact you directly, now that I'm off on a side track and probably out of your referral net. Let's talk soon—I'll move quickly if the opportunity you have is a good one. Then, I'll quickly repeat these successes for your client.

Sincerely,

Jane Swift

Jane Swift

JS

Broadcast Letter

JANE SWIFT

18 Central Park Street, Anytown, NY 14788
(516) 555-1212

(Date)

Emily _____
(Title)
ABC Corporation
1 Industry Plaza
Anytown, NY 12096

Dear Ms. _____:

As an independent contractor in secretarial services, I ask that you keep me in mind for vacation and leave of absence staff needs. Following a May commitment, my calendar is again open.

As vacation plan dates are firmed up and other staffing needs for secretarial services materialize, I would be pleased to discuss arrangements and confirm commitment dates with you.

I look forward to hearing from you. Please leave a message through the voice mail number above.

Very truly yours,

Jane Swift

Jane Swift

JS

POWER PHRASES

Consider using adaptations of these key phrases in your broadcast letters.

I hope this summary describes my experience and provides you with a better understanding of my capabilities. Thank you for your help.

Recently I read about the expansion of your company in the _____ Sun. As the _____ industry is of great interest to me, I was excited to learn of the new developments within ABC Corporation.

I feel confident that a short conversation about my experience and your growth plans would be mutually beneficial. I will be calling you early next week to follow up on this letter.

Currently, my total compensation package brings me in the low $70's; and I am looking for a company that rewards performance consistently.

I am available for relocation and travel and am targeting compensation in the $50K range.

I fervently request more than your cursory consideration, I request your time to verify my claims. YOUR TIME WILL NOT BE WASTED.

Superior recommendations from industry leaders as well as verifiable salary history is available.

I hope you will not think me presumptuous in writing directly to you; however, in view of your position, I am led to believe that you are more aware of your organization's telecommunications personnel requirements than anyone else.

I am confident that with my experience I can make a significant contribution to your organization.

I am a self-starter who is looking to join a reputable firm that could benefit from an individual who is ready to give 110%. With over three years of sales experience, I have developed excellent interpersonal, organizational and communication skills. I am a hard-working individual who is motivated by the knowledge that my earnings are directly related to the time, energy and effort that I commit to my position.

I am personable, present a highly professional image, and deal effectively with both peers and clientele. I am confident you will agree that I should be representing your firm and not your competition. My salary requirements are negotiable. I will call you this week to set up a mutually convenient time for an interview.

Since beginning with ABC Company, my average commission has progressed from $400 to $650 weekly. My current salary or commission requirement would range upwards of mid-$20Ks, with specifics flexible and negotiable.

I look forward to hearing from you in the near future to schedule an interview at your convenience, during which I hope to learn more about the position, your company's plans and goals, and how I can contribute to the success of your team.

Networking Letter

JAMES SHARPE

---

18 Central Park Street ♦ Anytown, NY 14788
(516) 555-1212

(Date)

Bob _____
(Title)
Krieger, Skvetney, Howell
Executive Search Consultants
2426 Foundation Road
Anytown, NY 14788

Dear Mr. _____:

We are members of the same professional association, the National Guild of Hospitality Marketing Professionals, and I need to call on your assistance. I have 16 years of business management experience in marketing and sales with premier package goods and service firms. My accomplishments include the revitalization of established brands, new product introduction, extensive advertising exposure, and marketing success in the fast food restaurant field.

Perhaps you know of a company that could use this scope of experience. In this regard, I enclose a copy of my resume outlining a few of my more significant accomplishments.

My objective is to find a director-level position at a marketing-driven company where my skills can contribute to the firm's growth and profitability. My preference would be to stay in an industry associated with consumer goods or services.

I am not limited by location and would consider the opportunity whenever it presents itself. My minimum salary requirement is in the upper $60K range and will depend on location and potential. You may use this figure for your own analysis. My preference is that you do not discuss salary with a potential employer.

Please advise me of any opportunities that I might investigate. Your assistance will be appreciated.

Sincerely yours,

James Sharpe

James Sharpe

JS
enclosure

Networking Letter

James Sharpe

18 Central Park Street, Anytown, NY 14788 ▪ (516) 555-1212

(Date)

Emily _____
(Title)
ABC Corporation
1 Industry Plaza
Anytown, NY 12096

Dear Ms. _____:

It was a pleasure to speak with you on the telephone recently and, even more so, to be remembered after all these years.

As mentioned during our conversation, I have just recently re-entered the job market and have ten years of experience with a 3,000-employee retail organization in the area of employee benefit administration. My experience includes pension plans, dental, life and disability insurance. I have been responsible for all facets of management of the company plan, including accounting, maintenance, and liaison with both staff and coverage providers.

My goal is to become a Benefits Manager in a larger organization with the possibility of advancement in other Human Resource areas. My preference is to remain in the Metropolitan _____ area.

For your information, enclosed is my resume. If any situations come to mind where you think my skills and background would fit or if you have any suggestions as to others with whom it might be beneficial for me to speak, I would appreciate hearing from you. I can be reached at the telephone numbers listed above.

Again, I very much enjoyed our conversation.

Yours truly,

James Sharpe

James Sharpe

JS
enclosure

Networking Letter

Jane Swift

18 Central Park Street, Anytown, NY 14788   ■   (516) 555-1212

(Date)

Phillip _____
(Title)
ABC Corporation
1 Industry Plaza
Anytown, NY 12096

Dear Mr. _____:

I met you a couple months ago at the _____ convention. Since that time I have been serving in the capacity of Project Coordinator/Administrator of a program at Children's Hospital. However, this program is federally funded for a limited time, and my position will soon be coming to an end.

I am looking for a position in management and would appreciate any assistance you could provide. Enclosed are both a resume and letter of recommendation for your review. As you will note from my resume, I have broad management experience in a number of areas. I particularly enjoy the development and implementation of new programs.

My skills and experience include:

- Extensive background in all areas of staff management, budget development, strategic planning, public relations, and marketing.
- Excellent communication skills.
- Demonstrated ability to approach management from a broad base of management experience in a number of areas. I particularly enjoy the development and implementation of new programs.
- Career experience complemented by a Master's Degree in Health Administration and a Bachelor's Degree in Social Work.

Thank you in advance for your assistance. I look forward to meeting with you again.

Sincerely,

Jane Swift

Jane Swift

JS
enclosure

Networking Letter

JAMES SHARPE
18 CENTRAL PARK STREET, AUSTIN, TX 55555, (516) 555-1212

(Date)

Emily _____
(Title)
ABC Corporation
1 Industry Plaza
Anytown, NH 12096

Dear Ms. _____:

It has been some months since I began my job search and one of my bigger challenges is getting the airline reservation agents to understand that I live in Austin, not Boston. It must be my Boston accent that fools them.

On a serious note, the opportunities in the computers and telecommunication industries are shrinking. Therefore, I need to expand my network of contacts to provide me greater exposure.

As you recall, I have over 20 years of sales and marketing experience ranging from _____ to Vice President of _____. The companies with which I have been affiliated have been _____, _____, _____ and _____.

I would greatly appreciate if you could provide me two new contracts for my network. Just note the name, company and phone number on the enclosed postcard. I will call them to make them aware of my availability and experiences should they hear of an opportunity.

Thanks for your continued assistance.

Sincerely,

James Sharpe

James Sharpe

JS
enclosure

119

Networking Letter

JAMES SHARPE
18 CENTRAL PARK STREET, ANYTOWN, NY 14788, (516) 555-1212

(Date)

Phillip _____
(Title)
ABC Corporation
1 Industry Plaza
Anytown, NY 12096

Dear Phil:

I was over at _____'s house a few weeks ago to pick up some information to aid me in my job search. You guessed it, Phil, I'm in transition. I was one of the many who was caught in _____'s downsizing a few weeks ago. As part of the information _____ gave me, _____'s newsletter was included.

I am not calling you or sending this letter to ask you for a job, but I could use your help in my job search. If you know of a position in your company or can give me any leads, I would appreciate it greatly. I'm sure you know how difficult it can be to develop a solid resume, job leads, interviews, etc. and with the local economic situation such that it is, the job of finding a job is compounded. I've included a copy of my resume for your reference and file.

I can be contacted at either my home phone number (555-1212) or at the _____ Outplacement Center at (555-1414). I will call you in a few days to follow up.

Sincerely,

James Sharpe

James Sharpe

JS
enclosure

Networking Letter

James Sharpe
18 Central Park Street, Anytown, NY 14788
(516) 555-1212

(Date)

Emily _____
(Title)
ABC Corporation
1 Industry Plaza
Anytown, NY 12096

Dear Ms. _____:

It was a pleasure to meet with you for lunch today. I am grateful for the time you took out of your busy schedule to assist me in my job search.

It was fascinating to learn about the new technology which is beginning to play a major role in the publishing field today. I have already been to the book store to purchase the book by _____ which you highly recommended I look forward to reading about his "space age" ideas.

I will be contacting _____ within the next few days to set up an appointment. I will let you know how things are progressing once I have met her.

Thanks again for your help. You will be hearing from me soon.

Yours sincerely,

James Sharpe

James Sharpe

JS

121

Networking Letter

JAMES SHARPE

18 Central Park Street   ◆   Anytown, NY 14788
(516) 555-1212

(Date)

Mr. Phillip _____
(Title)
ABC Corporation
1 Industry Plaza
Anytown, NY 12096

Dear Mr. _____:

It was good talking with you again. As promised, I am enclosing a copy of my resume for your information. If any appropriate opportunities come to your attention, I would appreciate it if you would keep me in mind.

I am looking for a Chief Operating, Administrative or Financial Officer position. During the eight years I have been with _____ as their Chief Financial Officer in North America, the business has grown from approximately $20 million to nearly $300 million. My responsibilities have included not only all the financial, treasury and systems operations but also very close liaison with store operations, distribution and Domestic sourcing. I am not restricting myself to the retail industry and, based on my prior experience at _____, would earnestly consider positions in other industries. I am particularly interested in an equity position.

In the right circumstances, I am prepared to relocate either domestically or overseas, with an opportunity to maximize my international expertise. I find the opportunities in Europe to be especially exciting, particularly the recent developments in Czechoslovakia. As indicated in my resume, I have spent three years in the London office of _____. I am fluent in Slovak and have familiarity with German.

After you have had a chance to look over the resume, please give me a call. Maybe we can even plan to get together sometime soon. In fact, my wife and I are considering going out your way with the _____ Club during October.

Best to you all.

Sincerely,

James Sharpe

James Sharpe

JS
enclosure

122

Networking Letter

JANE SWIFT

18 Central Park Street ◆ Anytown, NY 14788
(516) 555-1212

(Date)

Alice _____
(Title)
Kriege, Skvetney, Howell
Executive Search Consultants
2426 Foundation Road
Anytown, NY 14788

Dear Ms. _____:

Please find the enclosed copy of my most recent resume. As we discussed, I am beginning to put some "feelers" out in advance of the completion of my degree in December. I have worked very hard, and sacrificed a lot, in order to better my educational credentials. My GPA is currently a 3.8. I am certain that it will be a 3.9 when I graduate. I intend to further the process by passing the CPA (Certified Public Accountant) Exam in June. I have already applied to take the exam. In addition, I will begin work on my MBA in the fall.

I do not intend to target any specific type of job. I am open to most anything that my qualifications will fit. My only criteria are the following:

1. An employer who will reimburse me for at least a fair portion of my MBA program tuition and books.
2. A reasonable increase over my present salary.
3. A decent medical and dental plan.
4. An employer that allows its employees to grow within the organization. In other words, develops them for increased responsibility and upward mobility.

It sounds as if I'm asking for the world, but I know that situations like this exist. I also know that I have a lot to offer. I can guarantee that any employer who hires me will be more than pleased with my abilities and accomplishments.

I would appreciate any advice and/or referrals you might be able to give me.

Sincerely,

Jane Swift

Jane Swift

JS
enclosure

Networking Letter

JANE SWIFT

18 Central Park Street, Anytown, NY 14788
(516) 555-1212

(Date)

Mr. Phillip _____
(Title)
ABC Corporation
1 Industry Plaza
Anytown, NY 12096

Dear Mr. _____ :

_____ suggested that I contact you regarding employment opportunities.

After many years in the legal community, I have decided that a career change is due in order to use my interpersonal skills to their fullest. As you may know, a secretary/paralegal position offers little advancement unless you become a lawyer or move into the administrative areas. It is with this growth potential in mind that I desire to work with upper level management in a corporate environment as an administrative assistant or executive secretary.

I am enclosing for your review copies of my resume and letters of recommendation. I look forward to the opportunity of meeting with you at your convenience. I have recently resigned from _____ and may be contacted at my home phone number of 516-555-1212, or at the above address. Thank you.

Very truly yours,

Jane Swift

Jane Swift

JS
enclosure

POWER PHRASES

Consider using adaptations of these key phrases in your networking letters.

It was good talking with you again. As promised, I am enclosing a copy of my resume for your information. If any appropriate opportunities come to your attention, I would appreciate it if you would keep me in mind.

After you have had a chance to look over the resume, please give me a call.

I am beginning to put some "feelers" out in advance of the completion of my degree in December.

I do not intend to target any specific type of job. I am open to most anything that my qualifications will fit. My only criteria are the following:

I would appreciate any advice and/or referrals you might be able to give me.

I am looking for a position in management and would appreciate any assistance you could provide.

As always, it was good to talk with you. Your positive outlook is catching. I've been called the eternal optimist but I always feel more upbeat after a conversation with you.

Many thanks for the words of encouragement and taking the time from your busy schedule to help me. It truly is appreciated. I have never faced an unemployment situation like this before.

It was a pleasure to speak with you on the telephone recently and, even more so, to be remembered after all these years.

For your information, enclosed is my resume. If any situations come to mind where you think my skills and background would fit or if you have any suggestions as to others with whom it might be beneficial for me to speak, I would appreciate hearing from you. I can be reached at the telephone numbers listed above.

He assured me that he would pass my resume along to you; however, in the event that it has not reached you yet, I am enclosing another.

Perhaps you know of a company that could use this scope of experience. In this regard, I enclose a copy of my resume outlining a few of my more significant accomplishments.

My objective is to find a _____ level position at a marketing driven company where my skills can contribute to the firm's growth and profitability.

I am not limited by location and would consider the opportunity wherever it presents itself.

First of all, let me sincerely thank you for taking the time and trouble to return my call last Monday. I found our conversation informative, entertaining, and (alas) a little scary. Needless to say, I genuinely appreciate your prompt response and generous, helpful advice.

Again, a thousand thanks for your time and consideration. If I might ask you one last favor, could you please give me your opinion of the revision? A copy is, as usual, enclosed.

I am writing to you in response to our recent conversation over the telephone. I thank you for your time and your advice. It was most generous of you and sincerely appreciated. Please accept my apologies for invading your privacy. I anticipated an address for written correspondence from an answering service.

I look forward to hearing from you on your next visit to _____.

I hope you'll keep me in mind if you hear of anything that's up my alley!

I recently learned that your firm is well-connected with manufacturers in the _____ area and does quality work. We should talk soon since it's very likely we can help each other.

I'll be in the office all next week and look forward to hearing from you. 1 have alerted my secretary; she'll put your call right through.

_____ suggested that I contact you regarding employment opportunities.

After many years in the _____ community, I have decided that a career change is due in order to use my interpersonal skills to their fullest.

Follow-up Letter (after telephone contact)

JANE SWIFT

18 Central Park Street, Anytown, NY 14788
(516) 555-1212

(Date)

Phillip _____
(Title)
ABC Corporation
1 Industry Plaza
Anytown, NY 12096

Dear Mr. _____:

Thank you for returning my telephone call yesterday. It was a
pleasure speaking with you, and as promised, a copy of my resume
is enclosed. As I mentioned, I have been working in law firms
since the end of February, as well as working on weekends and in
the evenings for over one year. At present, I am looking for a
second or third shift to continue developing my word processing
and legal skills.

Although the majority of my positions have been more managerial
and less secretarial, I have developed strong office skills over
the years. While I was attending both undergraduate and graduate
school, I worked as Administrative Assistants to Deans and
Department Heads, in addition to working in other professional
capacities.

_____ speaks very highly of me, and if you need to confirm a
reference with him, please feel free to contact him at _____.
In addition, I would be happy to furnish you with names of people I
have worked for within law firms over the past year.

Within the next day, I will be contacting you to arrange a
convenient meeting time to discuss the position you now have
available. However, if you would like to speak with me, feel free
to contact me at 555-1212.

Thank you again for calling yesterday. I look forward to speaking
with you on the telephone, and meeting you in person.

Sincerely,

Jane Swift

Jane Swift

JS
enclosure

Follow-up Letter (after telephone contact)

JANE SWIFT
18 Central Park Street, Anytown, NY 14788
(516) 555-1212

(Date)

Emily _____
(Title)
ABC Corporation
1 Industry Plaza
Anytown, NY 12096

Dear Ms. _____:

I appreciate the time you took yesterday to discuss the position at _____. I recognize that timing and awareness of interest are very important in searches of this type. Your comment regarding an attempt to contact me earlier this summer is a case in point.

Enclosed, as you requested, you will find an outline resume. I also believe that my experiences as a director of physical plant services are readily transferable to a new environment. I believe that I can contribute a great deal to the satisfaction of your clients needs.

Realizing that letters and resumes are not entirely satisfactory means of judging a person's ability or personality, I suggest a personal interview to discuss further your client's needs and my qualifications. I can be reached directly or via message at (516)555-1212, so that we may arrange a mutually convenient time to meet. I look forward to hearing from you. Thank you for your time and consideration.

Sincerely,

Jane Swift

Jane Swift

JS
enclosure

Follow-up Letter (after telephone contact)

JAMES SHARPE

18 Central Park Street, Anytown, NY 14788 ■ (516) 555-1212

(Date)

Phillip _____
(Title)
ABC Corporation
1 Industry Plaza
Anytown, NY 12096

Dear Mr. _____ :

Thank you for taking the time recently to respond to my questions concerning a _____ position with _____, as advertised in _____ (October —, 19—). As you suggested, I have enclosed my resume for your review and consideration.

As you will find detailed on my resume, I offer nearly two years of sales experience, with over one year of successful advertising sales for a $1 million regional business publication.

Within one year, I have developed a formerly neglected territory from approximately $50,000 to its current $180,000 in annual sales.

I have an excellent track record in customer retention, account penetration, low receivables, and consistent goal achievement. I have had experience working with client advertising agencies and directly with smaller clients. I am confident that I can make similar contributions to your sales efforts, and would consider an interview with _____ to be a tremendous career opportunity.

As I have mentioned, I am relocating to your area in January and I would welcome the opportunity to discuss my background and accomplishments with you in further detail. I will be in your area Friday, December —th, and will call you early next week to see if we might schedule a meeting at that time.

Best regards,

James Sharpe

James Sharpe

JS
enclosure

Follow-up Letter (after telephone contact)

JANE SWIFT

18 CENTRAL PARK STREET, ANYTOWN, NY 14788, (516) 555-1212

(Date)

Emily _____
(Title)
ABC Corporation
1 Industry Plaza
Anytown, NY 12096

Dear Ms. _____:

Per yesterday's conversation, I am forwarding a copy of my resume and am looking forward to our meeting in the very near future.

As we discussed, the positions which interest me are as follows:

    Event/Arts Management
    Promotions/Advertising/Public Relations
    Corporate Training.

I am a fanatic over image, excellence, and attention to quality and detail. As my academic and career background reveal, I have the tenacity of a rat terrier when it comes to task accomplishment.

I have never held an '8-5' job and would most likely be bored to death if I had one. Therefore, I am looking for something fast-paced and challenging to my gray matter that will allow growth and advancement and an opportunity to learn. I am in my element when I am in a position to organize . . . the more details the better!

I'll give you a buzz on Tuesday, March —th to try to set an appointment for further discussion.

Sincerely,

Jane Swift

Jane Swift

JS
enclosure

Follow-up Letter (after telephone contact)

JAMES SHARPE

18 Central Park Street, Anytown, NY 14788   ■   (516) 555-1212

(Date)

Bob _____
(Title)
Krieger, Skvetney, Howell
Executive Search Consultants
2426 Foundation Road
Anytown, NY 14788

Dear Mr. _____:

In reference to our telephone conversation enclosed is my _____ resume. I believe the one you have is written towards a purchasing position.

Since we last spoke I have been working as a business consultant for the _____ group of companies on projects in a number of different areas outlined below.

- Elected to serve as the Vice Chairman of the _____ Chapter 11 bankruptcy creditors committee including the two primary subcommittees reviewing offers to purchase the _____ operations.
- Spearheaded and supervised upgrading of the _____ companies' communications systems, including printing and copy machines, telecommunications systems, computer hardware and software systems, computer scanning system, computer filing system, and fax and modem transmission systems.
- Set up and implemented an auto and entry floor mat marketing program for _____ including pricing and product displays for retail sales outlets.
- Researched, purchased and installed a bar code labeling program for the companies' products, including label set up and printing systems to allow them to sell their products to _____.
- Participated in the design and layout of a new logo for _____ division including specifications for all letterheads, forms and printed communications materials.
- Provided major input for a factory paid _____ point of sale system to display custom automotive floor mats.

Most of my projects should be wrapped up by the end of November and so I will be looking for another company who could utilize my broad range of experience. Please let me know if you think you might have something for me.

Sincerely,

James Sharpe

James Sharpe

JS
enclosure

Follow-up Letter (after telephone contact)

JAMES SHARPE
18 CENTRAL PARK STREET, ANYTOWN, NY 14788, (516) 555-1212

(Date)

Emily _____
(Title)
ABC Corporation
1 Industry Plaza
Anytown, NY 12096

Dear Ms. _____:

This letter is in response to our phone conversation this afternoon, and your ad in the _____ *Journal* regarding the _____ position available.

My background includes experience (sales and technical) with a wide range of computer systems, as well as with industrial distributed process control systems and measurement instrumentation. Considering the complexity of the equipment I've worked on and sold, most of the products being marketed will present no difficulty to me. The customer base would take a little time, but this would be nothing excessive.

I am a bright, articulate, and well-groomed professional with excellent telemarketing skills, sales instincts, and closing abilities. I would like to meet with you to discuss how I could contribute to the effectiveness and profitability of your operations.

Sincerely,

James Sharpe

James Sharpe

JS

Follow-up Letter (after telephone contact)

JAMES SHARPE

18 Central Park Street ◆ Anytown, NY 14788
(516) 555-1212

(Date)

Bob _____
(Title)
Krieger, Skvetney, Howell
Executive Search Consultants
2426 Foundation Road
Anytown, NY 14788

Dear Mr. _____:

As you will recall, we spoke about my qualifications for the opportunity with your New York client (account #5188) and you mentioned that you would be forwarding my resume for consideration.

I wanted you to have my updated resume, and I am enclosing several copies. I hope you'll send one to your client and keep the other for your own files. I'm aware that you have many business leads and that my qualifications might pertain to other opportunities—please remember me if something arises that would tie in with my background.

My experience in grocery and merchandising areas is considerable, and I have an extensive network of business contacts in the Pacific Northwest. My many long-term professional relationships would benefit any employer in this area.

I'd like to meet with you to tell you more about my background and to show you some of the training and marketing materials I 've developed. This would give you a better picture of my capabilities.

I'll be in touch with you in the near future to find out when we might get together. Thank you again for your consideration.

Sincerely yours,

James Sharpe

James Sharpe

JS
enclosures

Follow-up Letter (after telephone contact)

JAMES SHARPE
_____

18 Central Park Street, Anytown, NY 14788   ■   (516) 555-1212

(Date)

Alice _____
(Title)
Krieger, Skvetney, Howell
Executive Search Consultants
2426 Foundation Road
Anytown, NY 14788

Dear Ms. _____:

As you requested in our telephone conversation this morning, I am enclosing a copy of my resume for your perusal.

As you can see from my resume, I have some excellent secretarial experience. My years with _____ Company were the most enjoyable, and I would really like to get back into a corporate environment.

You asked about my salary history. At present, my salary is $1,820 per month. I started work for _____ two and a half years ago at $1,600 per month. My own business endeavors were only part-time, so I don't have a good figure to use here.

If you have any questions, or any marvelous positions you think I would be perfect for, please call me either at my home, (516) 555-1212, or at the office (discreetly, please), (516) 555-1213. I would be interested in meeting with you and discussing what possibilities exist. Thank you for your consideration.

Yours sincerely,

James Sharpe

James Sharpe

JS
enclosure

Follow-up Letter (after telephone contact)

James Sharpe

18 Central Park Street, Anytown, NY 14788 ▪ (516) 555-1212

(Date)

Bob _____
(Title)
Krieger, Skvetney, Howell
Executive Search Consultants
2426 Foundation Road
Anytown, NY 14788

Dear Mr. _____:

THANK YOU for allowing me to "tell you a little about myself." I have just completed my MBA (December, 19—) and would appreciate the opportunity to talk with your client companies who are in need of an experienced and seasoned manager. Whether the need is for general (operational) management, products, marketing, or sales, my substantial background in management, marketing and technical products should be very valuable to your clients.

I have enclosed two resumes (marketing oriented and operational oriented) with some other information which you may find useful. With eyes firmly welded to the bottom line, I offer; the ABILITY to manage, build and quickly understand their business, EXPERIENCE in domestic and international corporate cultures, INTELLIGENCE and the capacity to grasp essential elements, and the WILLINGNESS to work hard, travel and relocate.

Realizing that most of your clients aren't looking for VP's, I'm not necessarily looking for fancy titles (but I am promotable). What I am looking for is that special position which will offer not only a challenge, but a career opportunity with long-range potential. I know my successes will bring them (and me) rewards.

Resumes and letters are brief by their very nature and cannot tell the whole story. I will be happy to discuss with your client and you how my commitment to them will help solve their needs or problems and will definitely make good things happen! After all, isn't that the bottom line?

May we work together?

Very truly yours,

James Sharpe

James Sharpe

JS
enclosures

135

Follow-up Letter (after telephone contact)

JANE SWIFT

18 Central Park Street   ◆   Anytown, NY 14788
(516) 555-1212

(Date)

Alice _____
(Title)
Krieger, Skvetney, Howell
Executive Search Consultants
2426 Foundation Road
Anytown, NY 14788

Dear Ms. _____:

As per my telephone conversation with Stephanie of your office today, this letter will confirm our meeting on Friday, June 9, 19— at 2:00 pm.

Again, thank you for your flexibility and for working out this time for us to meet at my convenience.

I look forward to continuing the discussion we had over the telephone in greater detail.

Very sincerely yours,

Jane Swift

Jane Swift

JS

Follow-up Letter (after telephone contact)

James Sharpe
18 Central Park Street, Anytown, NY 14788
(516) 555-1212

(Date)

Emily _____
(Title)
ABC Corporation
1 Industry Plaza
Anytown, NY 12096

Dear Ms. _____:

I have enclosed my resume and a copy of a letter of recommendation.

I am sorry that it has taken me almost a week to get this information to you. At the beginning of last week I was finally able to get a policy changed, and thereby be eligible for overtime work with compensation. For the past week I have been working ten hour days, save for a rest on Sunday.

I am anxious to be interviewing for employment because the product I have been developing for the past two and half years no longer represents any opportunity for growth. Recently the company decided not to pursue sales of this product.

I consider that my employment may be curtailed when this product is no longer maintained and I would like to be in charge of my own departure date. I will be interested to hear more about the opportunities which you can present, and of course the terms set by your company. I presently earn $28.5K and would seek either immediate opportunity for growth or $30-$35K.

Thank you,

James Sharpe

James Sharpe

JS
enclosures

POWER PHRASES

Consider using adaptations of these key phrases in your follow-up letters after phone calls.

As you requested in our telephone conversation this morning, I am enclosing a copy of my resume for your perusal.

As you can see from my resume, I have some excellent secretarial experience.

I'll give you a buzz on Tuesday, March —th, to set an appointment for further discussion.

In reference to our telephone conversation, enclosed is my sales and marketing resume; I believe the one you have is written towards a purchasing position.

I am a bright, articulate, and well-groomed professional with excellent telemarketing skills, sales instincts, and closing abilities. I am seeking a dynamic position with a reputable firm. I would like to meet with you in person to discuss how I could contribute to the effectiveness of your clients' operations.

Again, thank you for your flexibility and for working out this time for us to meet at my convenience.

Please remember me if something arises that would tie in with my background.

My many long-term professional relationships would benefit any employer in this area.

I'd like to meet with you to tell you more about my background and to show you some of the training and marketing materials I've developed. This would give you a better picture of my capabilities.

As you suggested when we spoke last week, I have enclosed my resume for your review and consideration. I contacted you on the recommendation of _____ of _____, who thought that you may have an interest in my qualifications for a position in the near future.

I have long admired _____ for its innovations in the industry, and I would consider it a tremendous career opportunity to be associated with your organization.

Follow-up Letter (after face-to-face meeting)

JAMES SHARPE
18 CENTRAL PARK STREET, ANYTOWN, NY 14788, (516) 555-1212

(Date)

Bob _____
(Title)
Krieger, Skvetney, Howell
Executive Search Consultants
2426 Foundation Road
Anytown, NY 14788

Dear Mr. _____:

Thank you for meeting with me this morning. Our associate _____ assured me that a meeting with you would be productive and it was. I sincerely appreciate your counsel, insight and advice.

I have attached my resume for your review. I would appreciate any feedback you may have regarding effectiveness and strength. I understand you may not have any searches underway that would be suitable for me at this time, but I would appreciate any future considerations.

As we reviewed this morning, I seek and am qualified for senior MIS positions in medium to large high tech manufacturing or services business. I seek compensation in the $150,000 and above range and look to report directly to the business CEO. These requirements are somewhat flexible depending on a number of factors, especially potential of a new position. My family and I are willing to relocate to any area except New York City.

Please consider any associates, customers or friends who may have contacts that would be useful for me to meet with. I have learned how important networking is and will really appreciate some assistance from a professional like you.

Thanks again, _____, and please let me know if I can be of service to you. I wish you and your colleagues continued success and look forward to a business relationship in the future.

Best regards,

James Sharpe

JS
enclosure

Follow-up Letter (after face-to-face meeting)

Jane Swift

18 Central Park Street, Anytown, NY 14788   ■   (516) 555-1212

(Date)

Emily _____
(Title)
ABC Corporation
1 Industry Plaza
Anytown, NY 12096

Dear Ms. _____:

It was most pleasant to meet with you this past Wednesday. In addition to experiencing a very enjoyable and informative interview, I came away very enthusiastic about the position you are seeking to fill. After meeting _____, I can certainly understand that her leaving will create a void in your office setting. She exudes a rare charm and I am humbled to be considered a viable candidate to replace her.

The tour was especially great. I do appreciate your having extended that added favor to the interview. I am, of course, looking forward to hearing from you in a positive way. Being part of your office and the _____ team is, indeed, an enticing prospect. Please be assured that I am ready for any "start date" you select.

Very sincerely,

Jane Swift

Jane Swift

JS

Follow-up Letter (after face-to-face meeting)

Jane Swift
18 Central Park Street, Anytown, NY 14788
(516) 555-1212

(Date)

Phillip _____
(Title)
ABC Corporation
1 Industry Plaza
Anytown, NY 12096

Dear Mr. _____:

Thank you so much for the time you spent with me this past Wednesday. It was such a pleasure to meet both you and _____. The insight you provided regarding the details of the position was most valuable to me. It is evident what an important contribution you have made.

I hope _____'s consideration of candidates will result in our being together again soon.

Very sincerely,

Jane Swift

Jane Swift

JS

Follow-up Letter (after face-to-face meeting)

JANE SWIFT
---

18 Central Park Street, Anytown, NY 14788 ■ (516) 555-1212

(Date)

Emily _____
(Title)
ABC Corporation
1 Industry Plaza
Anytown, NY 12096

Dear Ms. _____:

Thank you for the opportunity to discuss the secretarial position.

ABC Corporation is involved in one of the most pressing concerns of today; environmentally safe methods of disposing of solid waste materials. The challenge of creating proper disposal system is paramount. I look forward to being a part of an organization that is focusing on furthering the technology needed to enhance our environment.

At ABC Corporation I would be able to:

- Be a productive assistant to management
- Be a part of a technologically developing industry
- Be in a position to learn and grow with the opportunities presented by that company
- Be involved in the excitement of a new expanding company

The skills that I have to offer ABC Corporation are:

- Professionalism, organization, and maturity
- Excellent office skills
- Ability to work independently
- A creative work attitude
- Research and writing skills
- Varied business background
- Willingness to learn

Again, thank you for considering my qualifications to become a part of your organization.

Sincerely,

Jane Swift

Jane Swift

JS

Follow-up Letter (after face-to-face meeting)

James Sharpe
18 Central Park Street, Anytown, NY 14788
(516) 555-1212

(Date)

Phillip _____
(Title)
ABC Corporation
1 Industry Plaza
Anytown, NY 12096

Dear Mr. _____:

The position we discussed Friday is a tremendously challenging one. After reviewing your comments about the job requirements, I am convinced that I can make an immediate contribution toward the growth and profitability of ABC Company.

Since you are going to reach a decision quickly, I would like to mention the following points which I feel qualify me for the job we discussed:

1. Proven ability to generate fresh ideas and creative solutions to difficult problems.
2. Experience in the area of program planning and development.
3. Ability to successfully manage many projects at the same time.
4. A facility for working effectively with people at all levels of management.
5. Experience in administration, general management and presentations.
6. An intense desire to do an outstanding job in anything which I undertake.

Thank you for the time and courtesy extended me. I will look forward to hearing from you.

Sincerely,

James Sharpe

James Sharpe

JS

Follow-up Letter (after face-to-face meeting)

JANE SWIFT

18 Central Park Street ◆ Anytown, NY 14788
(516) 555-1212

(Date)

Emily _____
(Title)
ABC Corporation
1 Industry Plaza
Anytown, NY 12096

Dear Ms. _____:

Gone but not forgotten . . .

Thank you for our time together this afternoon. What I lack in specific experience in your business I more than make up for with my people power, proven record of achievement, energy, and just pure tenacity.

You need someone who can handle new challenges without getting frazzled. I can pilot an airplane, conduct a class, build a campfire, emerge (unscathed) from _____ traffic, write a love story, swim a lap, sell a car, and I've even been to a goat roping!

Given the opportunity I can succeed in your office. That makes you and me both successes. Is that worth the investment in training me?

You know we can do it.

Call me!

Sincerely,

Jane Swift

Jane Swift

JS

Follow-up Letter (after face-to-face meeting)

James Sharpe

18 Central Park Street, Anytown, NY 14788   ■   (516) 555-1212

(Date)

Bob _____
(Title)
Krieger, Skvetney, Howell
Executive Search Consultants
2426 Foundation Road
Anytown, NY 14788

Dear Mr. _____:

It was a pleasure speaking with you regarding my search for a position in corporate graphic design. Thank you for your initial interest.

The position I am looking for is usually found in a corporate marketing or public relations department. The titles vary; Graphic Design Manager, Advertising Manager and Publications Director are a few. In almost every case the job description includes management and coordination of the corporation's printed marketing materials whether they are produced by in-house designers or by an outside advertising agency or design firm.

I would like to stay in the _____ area; at least, I would like to search this area first. My salary requirement is $_____ a year.

My professional experience, education, activities and skills uniquely qualify me for a position in Corporate Graphic Design. My portfolio documents over eight years of experience in the business, design, project consultation and supervision of quality printed material for a wide range of clients.

I hope you will keep me in your files for future reference. I will telephone your office next week to discuss my situation further.

Sincerely,

James Sharpe

James Sharpe

JS

145

Follow-up Letter (after face-to-face meeting)

JANE SWIFT

18 Central Park Street, Anytown, NY 14788
(516) 555-1212

(Date)

Alice _____
(Title)
Krieger, Skvetney, Howell
Executive Search Consultants
2426 Foundation Road
Anytown, NY 14788

Dear Ms. _____:

It was a pleasure meeting with you last week in your office. I appreciate the time you spent with me as well as the valuable information you offered. As we discussed, I have adjusted my resume in regards to my position with _____. I have included the new resume with this letter so that your files can be updated.

_____, please allow me to thank you again for the compliment on my ability to present a strong interview. Please keep this in mind when considering me for placement with one of your clients.

Sincerely,

Jane Swift

Jane Swift

JS
enclosure

Follow-up Letter (after face-to-face meeting)

JAMES SHARPE

18 Central Park Street, Anytown, NY 14788   ▪   (516) 555-1212

(Date)

Phillip _____
(Title)
ABC Corporation
1 Industry Plaza
Anytown, NY 12096

Dear Mr. _____ :

I would like to take this opportunity to thank you for the interview Wednesday morning at _____, and to confirm my strong interest in an entry-level position with your company.

As we discussed, I feel that my education and background have provided me with an understanding of business operations which will prove to be an asset to your company. Additionally, I have always been considered a hard worker and a dependable, loyal employee. I am confident that I can make a valuable contribution to your Group Pension Fund area.

I look forward to meeting with you again in the near future to further discuss your needs.

Sincere regards,

James Sharpe

James Sharpe

JS

Follow-up Letter (after face-to-face meeting)

JAMES SHARPE

18 Central Park Street   ◆   Anytown, NY 14788
(516) 555-1212

(Date)

Emily _____
(Title)
ABC Corporation
1 Industry Plaza
Anytown, NY 12096

Dear Ms. _____:

I enjoyed our meeting on Monday, December —, 19—. I was greatly
impressed with you and your company. Thank you for taking the
time to discuss the duties and responsibilities of the position.

From our conversation, I feel confident in my ability to reach
and exceed your expectations. I have a positive attitude and a
solid track record that proves I have surpassed high quotas at
_____. In addition, my two years of cold calling sales
experience and my strong closing skills, will be an asset to your
firm.

I am looking forward to spending a day in the field with an ABC
representative. I will telephone you later this week to set up an
appointment for my second interview.

Sincerely,

James Sharpe

James Sharpe

JS

Follow-up Letter (after face-to-face meeting)

JANE SWIFT

18 Central Park Street, Anytown, NY 14788
(516) 555-1212

(Date)

Phillip _____
(Title)
ABC Corporation
1 Industry Plaza
Anytown, NY 12096

Dear Mr. _____:

Thank you for allowing me the opportunity to meet with you to discuss the EDP Audit position currently available at ABC Company. The position sounds very challenging and rewarding with ample room for growth. I feel my background and qualifications prepare me well for the EDP audit position we discussed.

I have a great willingness and eagerness to learn more about EDP auditing, and feel that I am the type of individual that would blend in well with the EDP audit staff at ABC Company. I look forward to hearing from you.

Sincerely,

Jane Swift

Jane Swift

JS

POWER PHRASES

Consider using adaptations of these key phrases in your follow-up letters after
face-to-face meetings.

Thank you for meeting with me this morning. Our associate _____ assured
me that a meeting with you would be productive and it was. I sincerely appreciate your counsel, insight and advice.

I have attached my resume for your review. I would appreciate any feedback
you may have regarding effectiveness and strength. I understand you may not
have any searches underway that would be suitable for me at this time, but I
would appreciate any future considerations.

Please consider any associates, customers, or friends who may have contacts
that would be useful for me to meet with. I have learned how important "networking" is and will really appreciate some assistance from a professional
like you.

Thanks again, _____, and please let me know if I can be of service to
you. I wish you and your colleagues continued success and look forward to a
business relationship in the future.

In addition to experiencing a very enjoyable and informative interview, I
came away very enthusiastic about the position you are seeking to fill.

I hope _____'s consideration of candidates will result in our being
together again soon.

During my drive home I savored the possibility of working for _____ in
the _____ area, and I must say it was an extremely pleasing thought.

I look forward to meeting with you again and hope our discussion will precede
a long-term working relationship.

I am looking forward to meeting _____ on August — at 10:00am, at which
time I will convince her of my abilities and prove I am the most qualified
person for the position.

It was a pleasure meeting with you lost week in your office. I appreciate the
time you spent with me as well as the valuable information you offered.

I hope you will take a few moments to review my resume and keep it in your
files for future reference. I will telephone your office next week to discuss
my situation further.

Gone but not forgotten . . .

Thank you for our time together this afternoon. What I lack in specific experience in your business I more than make up for with my people power and my
proven record of achievement, energy, and just pure tenacity.

Given the opportunity, I can succeed in your office. That makes you and me both successes. Is that worth the investment in training me?

I would like to take this opportunity to thank you for the interview this morning, and to express my strong interest in the position with _____.

I would welcome the opportunity to apply and to further develop my talents within your company. Through my conversations with you and Mr. _____, I felt that the company provides exactly the type of career opportunity that I am seeking, and I am confident that I will prove to be an asset to your organization.

I trust our meeting this morning helped you further define the position. First and foremost, however, I hope that you came away from our meeting with a vision that includes me filling one of the many offices in _____. I certainly did.

I would like to take this opportunity to thank you for the interview on Thursday morning. I was very impressed with the operation and I am enthused about the prospects of joining your team.

Since we spent so much time discussing the subject, I have enclosed . . .

I look forward to hearing from you again to further discuss the position. Through my conversations with you and _____, I felt . . .

After reviewing your comments about the job requirements, I am convinced that I can make an immediate contribution toward the growth and profitability of _____.

Since you are going to reach a decision quickly, I would like to mention the following points which I feel qualify me for the job we discussed:

The position in the _____ area is very attractive to me.

The interview confirmed that I want this career opportunity. Specifically, I want to work in the _____ department for you and _____. That is the simplest way to say it. I will call you this week to see what the next step is in the process.

Again, thank you for your time and interest.

It was indeed a pleasure to meet with you after working with you by telephone several years ago.

Thank you for taking time out of your busy schedule to meet with me on Tuesday December —, 19—. I left the interview with an extremely favorable impression of your company.

I would like to take this opportunity to thank you for the interview on Friday morning, and to confirm my strong interest in the _____ position.

A career opportunity with _____ Corporation is particularly appealing because of its solid reputation and track record in research and development.

I am confident that the training program and continued sales support will provide me with the background that I need to succeed in a _____ career.

I look forward to discussing my background and the position with you in greater detail.

I want to take this opportunity to thank you for the interview on Tuesday afternoon, and to confirm my strong interest in the position of _____ with XYZ Health Care Agency.

From our conversation, I feel confident in my ability to reach and exceed your expectations.

I am looking forward to spending a day in the field with a _____ representative. I will telephone you later this week to set up an appointment for my second interview.

Thank you for the time during my visit to _____ yesterday. I enjoyed our conversation at lunch and learned more about personal trust and investment services.

Thank you for your time and interest today. As I indicated, I am very new to this game of searching for employment and it is nice to start this effort on a positive note.

I am eager to hear from you concerning your decision; I know that you have several other candidates to meet with, so I will wait patiently. Good luck to you in your interview process, I know they must be difficult. Again, thank you so much for your time and consideration. I would welcome the opportunity to work for your company.

_____, the visit with you left me feeling positive about the possibility of working for _____. I would appreciate an opportunity to join your staff, and look forward to hearing from you.

"Resurrection" Letter

JANE SWIFT
18 Central Park Street, Anytown, NY 14788
(516) 555-1212

(Date)

Phillip _____
(Title)
ABC Corporation
1 Industry Plaza
Anytown, NY 12096

Dear Mr. _____:

I understand from _____ of _____ that the search is continuing for the Wholesale Market Manager position at _____ Bank & Trust. As you continue your search, I would like to ask that you keep in mind the following accomplishments and experiences that I would bring to the job:

1. Maximized relationships and increased balances through the sale of trust and cash management products.
2. Captured largest share of public funds market in _____ within three years and captured a disproportionate market share of insurance companies in _____.
3. Developed cash management and trust products tailored to the needs of my target market.
4. Marketed services through mass mailings and brochures, through planning and conducting industry-specific seminars, and through active participation in target market's industry professional organization.
5. Direct experience in all phases of wholesale commercial banking, including: market segmentation, prospecting, building and maintaining customer relationships, lending, and the sale of non-credit products and services.

Sincerely,

Jane Swift

Jane Swift

JS

P.S. I will call you next week, after you have seen the other candidates, to continue our discussion. In the meantime, please be assured of both my competency and commitment.

"Resurrection" Letter

James Sharpe

18 Central Park Street, Anytown, NY 14788 ▪ (516) 555-1212

(Date)

Alice _____
(Title)
Krieger, Skvetney, Howell
Executive Search Consultants
2426 Foundation Road
Anytown, NY 14788

Dear Ms. _____:

I am writing to you to follow up on the initial inquiry I wrote to you on July —th, 19—. At that time I forwarded you a cover letter and resume. I am in the construction management and business management fields. Since I have not had a response I can only assume that you do not have any currently active searches that meet my qualifications in process or that my file has been deactivated.

I am still in the market for an executive position which matches my qualifications and abilities. I am open to relocating throughout the United States and overseas. If there are any positions that become available, I would be interested in hearing from you. If you need an updated resume, please write or call me and I would be most happy to forward you any information required.

Sincerely,

James Sharpe

James Sharpe

JS

P.S. I'll call in a couple of days to follow up on this letter.

"Resurrection" Letter

Jane Swift

18 Central Park Street, Anytown, NY 14788 ▪ (516) 555-1212

(Date)

Phillip _____
(Title)
ABC Corporation
1 Industry Plaza
Anytown, NY 12096

Dear Mr. _____:

I wanted to thank you for the interview we had on March —th, 19—. The position that was being offered sounds like something I would be interested in. However I do understand your reasons for not choosing me for the position and I thank you very much for your honesty.

Perhaps when you are looking for an account executive with five years of experience instead of ten, you will bear me in mind. I am determined to be your choice. I hope the fact that I came in a close second to someone with twice my chronological experience will help you keep me in mind.

I look forward to hearing from you, and thank you again for your time. With your permission I will stay in touch.

Sincerely,

Jane Swift

Jane Swift

JS

"Resurrection" Letter

JAMES SHARPE
18 CENTRAL PARK STREET, ANYTOWN, NY 14788, (516) 555-1212

(Date)

Emily _____
(Title)
ABC Corporation
1 Industry Plaza
Anytown, NY 12096

Dear Ms. _____:

I must have been one of the first people you spoke with about the ad because at the time you seemed very interested in me. However, when I called you back, you had received so many calls for the position, you didn't know one from the other. That's understandable, so I hope I can stir your memory and more importantly your interest.

When I spoke with you I got the feeling we could both benefit from working together. I am a computer enthusiast, always looking for new applications and ideas to implement on the computer. I have a solid programming and project development background in both the DOS and Macintosh worlds. What's even better is my hobby: my work. I spend countless hours in one way or another doing things which concern computing.

You had asked if I had children and I do. A four-and- a-half-year-old daughter, and a four-and-a-half-month-old daughter. You had some ideas for children's software, and thought having kids would help when working on such software. My oldest uses _____ on my Macintosh at home and double-clicks away, without any assistance from my wife or myself. She has learned a great deal from "playing" with it and is already more computer literate than I ever expected. We need more software like _____ to help stir the minds of our kids.

I have enclosed a resume for your perusal. But in case you don't want to read all the details, here it is in short:

- I have 6 years programming and development experience in DOS.
- I have 3 years programming and development experience on the Macintosh.
- I am currently the Senior Developer for Macintosh programming here at _____ Corp.

I look forward to speaking with you again, so please don't hesitate to call me, either at home (516-555-1212) or at work (516-555-1213) anytime.

Regards,

James Sharpe

James Sharpe

JS
enclosure

156

"Resurrection" Letter

JANE SWIFT

18 Central Park Street, Anytown, NY 14788   ▪   (516) 555-1212

(Date)

Bob _____
(Title)
Krieger, Skvetney, Howell
Executive Search Consultants
2426 Foundation Road
Anytown, NY 14788

Dear Mr. _____:

I feel I should more thoroughly explain why I am willing to take even an entry level position considering all my past experience. And that's just it—past experience.

For the past three years I ran my own small business, which, of course, kept me out of the job market. Meanwhile, computers took over the world! Fortunately, since moving here and doing temp jobs, have gotten hands-on experience in data entry. I have also taken and finished a private course in WordPerfect 5.0. So I guess that makes me computer literate if not entirely experienced.

Nevertheless, I'm in no position to be proud or disdainful of clerical jobs, as I realize I must start somewhere. Fortunately, I enjoy all facets of office work (even filing), so that would not be a problem. I have enough faith in myself and my ability to learn quickly to know that some form of upper movement would be possible for me . . . eventually.

Incidentally, even though I am on a temp job this week and possibly next, I do have an answering machine I check every couple of hours during the day. So please leave a message and I'll return your call soon after.

Thank you and I look forward to hearing from you. I have enclosed another copy of my resume for you.

Sincerely,

Jane Swift

Jane Swift

JS
enclosure

"Resurrection" Letter

James Sharpe
18 Central Park Street, Anytown, NY 14788
(516) 555-1212

(Date)

Alice _____
(Title)
Krieger, Skvetney, Howell
Executive Search Consultants
2426 Foundation Road
Anytown, NY 14788

Dear Ms. _____:

Four months ago you and I discussed an opportunity at Active Products, and you were kind enough to set up meetings with _____ and _____. Shortly thereafter, as you know, I accepted a position with _____, where I am now.

For reasons I will go into when we meet, I would like to re-open our discussions. If you think such a conversation would be mutually beneficial. I hope we can get together. I'll call next week to see when you have a half hour or so of free time.

Sincerely,

James Sharpe

James Sharpe

JS

POWER PHRASES

Consider using adaptations of these key phrases in your resurrection letters.

I turned down your job, but for reasons I will go into when we meet, I would like to re-open our discussions. If you think such a conversation would be mutually beneficial I hope we can get together. I'll call next week to see when you have a half hour or so of free time.

As you continue your search, I would like to ask that you keep in mind the following accomplishments and experiences that I would bring to the job.

I am still in the market for an executive position which matches my qualifications and abilities. I am open to relocating through the United States and overseas. If there are any positions that become available, I would be interested in hearing from you.

I look forward to hearing from you, and thank you again for your time. With your permission I will stay in touch.

I hope I can stir your memory and, more importantly, your interest.

I look forward to speaking with you again, so please don't hesitate to call me either at home or at work anytime.

Nevertheless, I'm in no position to be proud or disdainful of clerical jobs as I realize I must start somewhere. Fortunately, I enjoy all facets of office work (even filing), so that would not be a problem. I have enough faith in myself and my ability to learn quickly to know that some form of upper movement would be possible for me . . . eventually.

Incidentally, even though I am on a temp job this week and possibly next, I do have an answering machine I check every couple of hours during the day. So please leave a message and I'll return your call soon after.

Rejection of Offer Letter

Jane Swift
18 Central Park Street, Anytown, NY 14788
(516) 555-1212

(Date)

Phillip _____
(Title)
ABC Corporation
1 Industry Plaza
Anytown, NY 12096

Dear Mr. _____:

It was indeed a pleasure meeting with you and your staff to discuss your needs for a
_____. Our time together was most enjoyable and informative.

As we have discussed during our meetings, I believe a purpose of preliminary interviews
is to explore areas of mutual interest and to assess the fit between the individual and the
position. After careful consideration, I have decided to withdraw from consideration for
the position.

My decision is based upon the fact that I have accepted a position elsewhere which is very
suited to my qualifications and experiences.

I want to thank you for interviewing me and giving me the opportunity to learn more
about your facility. You have a fine team and I would have enjoyed working with you.

Best wishes to you and your staff.

Sincerely,

Jane Swift

Jane Swift

JS

Rejection of Offer Letter

JAMES SHARPE

18 Central Park Street, Anytown, NY 14788 ▪ (516) 555-1212

(Date)

Emily _____
(Title)
ABC Corporation
1 Industry Plaza
Anytown, NY 12096

Dear Ms. _____:

I would like to take this opportunity to thank you for the interview on Thursday morning, and to express my strong interest in future employment with your organization.

While I appreciate very much your offer for the position of Department Manager, I feel that at this stage of my career I am seeking greater challenges and advancement than the Department level is able to provide. Having worked in _____ management for over four years, I am confident that my skills will be best applied in a position with more responsibility and accountability.

As we discussed, I look forward to talking with you again in January about how I might contribute to ABC Corporation in the capacity of Unit Manager.

Sincere regards,

James Sharpe

James Sharpe

JS

POWER PHRASES

Consider using adaptations of these key phrases in your rejection of offer letters.

It was indeed a pleasure meeting with you and your staff to discuss your needs for a _____. Our time together was most enjoyable and informative.

After careful consideration, I have decided to withdraw from consideration for the position.

As we discussed, I look forward to talk with you again in _____ about how I might contribute to _____ in the capacity of _____.

Acceptance Letter

```
                        JAMES SHARPE
         _____

         18 Central Park Street    ◆    Anytown, NY 14788
                        (516) 555-1212




                                              (Date)




         Phillip _____
         (Title)
         ABC Corporation
         1 Industry Plaza
         Anytown, NY 12096

         Dear Mr. _____:

              I would like to express my appreciation for your letter
         offering me the position of _____ in your _____
         Department at a starting salary of $4,695 per month.

              I was very impressed with the personnel and facilities at
         your refinery in _____ and am writing to confirm my
         acceptance of your offer. If it is acceptable with you I will
         report to work on November —th, 19—.

              Let me once again express my appreciation for your offer and
         my excitement about joining your engineering staff. I look
         forward to my association with ABC Corporation and feel my
         contributions will be in line with your goals of growth and
         continued success for the company.

                                   Sincerely,

                                   James Sharpe

                                   James Sharpe


         JS
```

163

Acceptance Letter

James Sharpe

18 Central Park Street, Anytown, NY 14788   ■   (516) 555-1212

(Date)

Emily _____
(Title)
ABC Corporation
1 Industry Plaza
Anytown, NY 12096

Dear Ms. _____:

This letter will serve as my formal acceptance of your offer to join your firm as Vice President of _____. I understand and accept the conditions of employment which you explained in your recent letter.

I will contact your personnel department this week to request any paperwork I might complete for their records prior to my starting date. Also, I will schedule a physical examination for insurance purposes. I would appreciate your forwarding any reading material you feel might hasten my initiation into the affairs of _____.

Yesterday I tendered my resignation at _____ and worked out a mutually acceptable notice time of four weeks, which should allow me ample time to finalize my business and personal affairs here, relocate my family, and be ready for work at _____ on schedule.

You, your board, and your staff have been most professional and helpful throughout this hiring process. I anxiously anticipate joining the ABC team and look forward to many new challenges. Thank you for your confidence and support.

Yours truly,

James Sharpe

James Sharpe

JS

Acceptance Letter

JANE SWIFT
18 CENTRAL PARK STREET, ANYTOWN, NY 14788, (516) 555-1212

(Date)

Phillip _____
Personnel Director
ABC Corporation
1 Industry Plaza
Anytown, NY 12096

Dear Mr. _____ :

This morning, I formally accepted ABC Corporation's employment offer in a fax to me at my home and submitted a resignation to my managers at _____. We are still working out the terms of my departure from _____, but it is safe to say that I will report to ABC Corporation no later than November —, 19—. It should be possible to confirm a starting date early tomorrow morning. I will telephone you directly when my erstwhile managers and I have a departure schedule completed.

_____ has scheduled my pre-employment physical for November —th and I do not expect any problems to arise. I have found several possible housing alternatives that I will be investigating, and I do not expect any problems here, either.

I appreciate the confidence you demonstrated by selecting me to be ABC's _____. I look forward to fulfilling your expectations in the coming years.

Sincerely,

Jane Swift

Jane Swift

JS

Acceptance Letter

JAMES SHARPE

18 Central Park Street, Anytown, NY 14788   ▪   (516) 555-1212

(Date)

Emily _____
(Title)
ABC Corporation
1 Industry Plaza
Anytown, NY 12096

Dear Ms. _____:

I would like to thank you and Mr. _____ for the interview on June —th. I would also like to thank you for choosing me as your candidate for the position. I am confident that you made an excellent choice.

I feel that I can achieve excellent results for your firm and I am looking forward to working with you. I am also anxious to get to know you and your corporation better.

Sincerely,

James Sharpe

James Sharpe

JS

Acceptance Letter

JANE SWIFT

18 Central Park Street ◆ Anytown, NY 14788
(516) 555-1212

(Date)

Phillip _____
(Title)
ABC Corporation
1 Industry Plaza
Anytown, NY 12096

Dear Mr. _____:

I am delighted to accept ABC Corporation's generous offer to
become your _____. All of the terms in your letter of
October 13th are amenable to me.

My resignation was submitted to the appropriate managers at
_____ this morning, but we are still working out the terms
of my departure. It should be possible to confirm a starting date
late today or early tomorrow. In any event, I will take the
pre-employment physical this Saturday morning, October —th.

I am eagerly anticipating starting my new position, particularly
at a firm with ABC Corporation's reputation. During the interim,
I will stay in direct contact with _____ to assure a smooth
initiation at ABC Corporation. Thank you again for this
opportunity.

Sincerely,

Jane Swift

Jane Swift

JS

POWER PHRASES

Consider using adaptations of these key phrases in your acceptance letters.

I am delighted to accept _____'s generous offer to become their _____. All of the terms in your letter of October 13th are amenable to me.

My resignation was submitted to the appropriate managers at _____ this morning, but we are still working out the terms of my departure.

I am genuinely anticipating starting my new position, particularly at a firm with _____'s reputation. During the interim, I will stay in direct contact with _____ to assure a smooth initiation at _____. Thank you again for this opportunity.

We are still working out the terms of my departure from _____, but it is safe to say that I will report to _____ no later than November —th. It should be possible to confirm a starting date early tomorrow morning. I will telephone you directly when my erstwhile managers and I have a departure schedule completed.

_____ has scheduled my pre-employment physical for _____, and I do not expect any problems to arise. I have found several possible housing alternatives that I will be investigating and I do not expect any problems here, either.

I appreciate the confidence you demonstrated by selecting me to be _____.

I am confident that you made an excellent choice.

I feel that I can achieve excellent results for your firm and I am looking forward to working with you. I am also anxious to get to know you and your corporation better.

This letter will serve as my formal acceptance of your offer to join _____. I understand and accept the conditions of employment which you explained in your recent letter.

I will contact your personnel department this week to request any paperwork I might complete for their records prior to my starting date. Also, I will schedule a physical examination for insurance purposes. I would appreciate your forwarding any reading material you feel might hasten my initiation into the affairs of _____.

Yesterday I tendered my resignation at _____ and worked out a mutually acceptable notice time of four weeks, which should allow me ample time to finalize my business and personal affairs here, relocate my family, and be ready for work at _____ on schedule.

You, your board, and your staff have been most professional and helpful throughout this hiring process. I anxiously anticipate joining the _____ team and look forward to many new challenges. Thank you for your confidence and support.

I look forward to making a contribution as part of your team.

I look forward to the challenges and responsibility of working in this position.

Resignation Letter

James Sharpe

18 Central Park Street   ◆   Anytown, NY 14788
(516) 555-1212

(Date)

Phillip _____
(Title)
ABC Corporation
1 Industry Plaza
Anytown, NY 12096

Dear Mr. _____:

Please accept this as two weeks formal notice of my resignation from the employ of ABC Corporation. My final day of employment will be August —, 19—.

I have thoroughly enjoyed the work environment and professional atmosphere at _____. Your management, direction, guidance and counseling have been the source of great personal and career satisfaction, and I am grateful. The experience and knowledge gained during my association with _____ has provided significant career growth for which I shall always be appreciative.

Once again, thank you for past consideration.

Very truly yours,

James Sharpe

James Sharpe

JS

Resignation Letter

18 Central Park Street
Anytown, NY 14788

(Date)

Emily _____
(Title)
ABC Corporation
1 Industry Plaza
Anytown, NY 12096

Dear Ms. _____:

I have deeply appreciated the past _____ years with ABC Corporation. These years have made a considerable contribution to my career and professional development and I hope that I have likewise contributed during this time to the growth and development of ABC Corporation. I am grateful for the kind of associates I have had the opportunity to work with, and the substantial support I have consistently received from management.

In order to continue this same progression of professional growth, I wish to formally communicate that I have already accepted a new position which I believe will significantly contribute to my continued career development.

_____, in order to further assure our continued longstanding relationship, I wish to strongly communicate my intentions to be as helpful as possible in this transition and in the transference of current responsibilities to those who will be assigned to these tasks. My final day with ABC Corporation will be June —th.

Sincerely,

Jane Swift

Jane Swift

JS

Resignation Letter

JANE SWIFT

18 Central Park Street ◆ Anytown, NY 14788
(516) 555-1212

(Date)

Phillip _____
(Title)
ABC Corporation
1 Industry Plaza
Anytown, NY 12096

Dear Mr. _____:

Please accept this as two (2) weeks formal notice of my resignation from the employ of ABC Corporation. My final date of employment will be March —, 19—.

I have thoroughly enjoyed the work environment and professional atmosphere here. Your management, direction, guidance and counseling have been the source of great personal and career satisfaction to me.

The experience and knowledge gained during my association with ABC has provided significant career growth for which I shall always be appreciative.

Sincerely,

Jane Swift

Jane Swift

JS

Resignation Letter

18 Central Park Street
Anytown, NY 14788

(Date)

Emily _____
(Title)
ABC Corporation
1 Industry Plaza
Anytown, NY 12096

Dear Ms. _____:

It is with sincere gratitude for my years of employment and many
fond memories that I am resigning from ABC Corporation. I must
leave no later than November —, 19—, but I would appreciate
leaving earlier if possible. Later today I will review my
programs' current status and develop a plan for their orderly and
seamless transition.

I have worked for five years with some of the most professional
_____ and managers in the _____ industry while here at
ABC Corporation. This has left an indelible impression on me, and
I would like to thank you for providing me with this fine
opportunity.

Sincerely,

James Sharpe

James Sharpe

JS

173

Resignation Letter

18 Central Park Street
Anytown, NY 14788

(Date)

Phillip _____
(Title)
ABC Corporation
1 Industry Plaza
Anytown, NY 12096

Dear Mr. _____:

Please accept my resignation of my position as Sales Representative in the _____ area, effective January —, 19—. I am offering two weeks' notice so that my territory can be effectively serviced during the transition, with the least amount of inconvenience to our clients.

While I have enjoyed very much working under your direction, I find now that I have an opportunity to further develop my career in areas that are more in line with my long term goals. I thank you for the sales training that I have received under your supervision. It is largely due to the excellent experience I gained working for ABC Sales Organization that I am now able to pursue this growth opportunity.

During the next two weeks, I am willing to help you in any way to make the transition as smooth as possible. This includes assisting in recruiting and training my replacement in the _____ territory. Please let me know if there is anything specific that you would like me to do.

Again, it has been a pleasure working as a part of your group.

Best regards,

James Sharpe

James Sharpe

JS

Resignation Letter

JANE SWIFT

18 Central Park Street, Anytown, NY 14788
(516) 555-1212

(Date)

Emily _____
(Title)
ABC Corporation
1 Industry Plaza
Anytown, NY 12096

Dear Ms. _____ :

As of this date, I am formally extending my resignation as _____ . I have accepted a position as Vice President of _____ at a university medical center in _____ .

My decision to leave ABC Corporation was made after long and careful consideration of all factors affecting the institution, my family, and my career. Although I regret leaving many friends here, I feel that the change will be beneficial to all parties. My subordinate staff is readily able to handle the institution's operations until you find a suitable replacement. I intend to finalize my business and personal affairs here over the next several weeks and will discuss a mutually acceptable termination date with you in person.

Finally, I can only express my sincere appreciation to you and the entire board for all your support, cooperation, and encouragement over the past several years. I will always remember my stay at ABC Corporation for the personal growth it afforded and for the numerous friendships engendered.

Yours truly,

Jane Swift

Jane Swift

JS

POWER PHRASES

Consider using adaptations of these key phrases in your resignation letters.

I am offering two weeks' notice so that my territory can be effectively serviced during the transition, with the least amount of inconvenience to our clients.

While I have enjoyed very much working under your direction, I find now that I have an opportunity to further develop my career in areas that are more in line with my long term goals. I thank you for the sales training that I have received under your supervision. It is largely due to the excellent experience I gained working for XYZ Sales Organization that I am now able to pursue this growth opportunity.

During the next two weeks, I am willing to help you in any way to make the transition as smooth as possible. This includes assisting in recruiting and training my replacement in the _____ territory. Please let me know if there is anything specific that you would like me to do.

Again, it has been a pleasure working as a part of your sales force.

I have thoroughly enjoyed the work environment and professional atmosphere at _____. Your guidance and counseling have been the source of great personal and career satisfaction, and I am grateful.

These _____ years have made a considerable contribution to my career and professional development and I hope that I have likewise contributed during this time to the growth and development of _____ Company. I am grateful for the kind of associates I have had the opportunity to work with, and the substantial support I have consistently received from management.

Thank-you Letter (after hire)

JAMES SHARPE

18 Central Park Street ◆ Anytown, NY 14788
(516) 555-1212

(Date)

Alice _____
(Title)
Krieger, Skvetney, Howell
Executive Search Consultants
2426 Foundation Road
Anytown, NY 14788

Dear Ms. _____:

I am happy to inform you that I received and accepted an offer of employment just after Thanksgiving. I am now employed by the _____ Corporation.

I would also like to thank you for all your help the past several months not only in my search for employment, but also by your understanding and friendly words of encouragement.

My duties include responsibility of all Dunn and Bradstreet software (General Ledger, Accounts Payable, Accounts Receivable, Fixed Assets, and Millinium) for _____ worldwide plus the first year training of several entry level employees.

I am enjoying my new responsibility and being fully employed again, although at times I feel overwhelmed with all I have to learn.

If there is ever anything I can do for you please call me. I hope you and your family have a wonderful holiday season and much luck and happiness in the new year.

Sincerely,

James Sharpe

James Sharpe

JS

Thank-you Letter (after hire)

JAMES SHARPE
18 CENTRAL PARK STREET, ANYTOWN, NY 14788, (516) 555-1212

(Date)

Phillip _____
(Title)
ABC Corporation
1 Industry Plaza
Anytown, NY 12096

Dear Mr. _____:

    I want you to be among the first to know that my job search has come to a very successful conclusion. I have accepted the position of _____ Director at _____, Inc. located in _____.

    I appreciate all the help and support you have provided over the last several months. It has made the job search process much easier for me. I look forward to staying in contact with you. Please let me know if I can be of any assistance to you in the future.

                Thank you,

                James Sharpe

                James Sharpe

JS

Thank-you Letter (after hire)

JAMES SHARPE

18 Central Park Street, Anytown, NY 14788 ▪ (516) 555-1212

(Date)

Phillip _____
(Title)
ABC Corporation
1 Industry Plaza
Anytown, NY 12096

Dear Mr. _____:

I am pleased to be able to let you know that I have accepted a position as a partner of
_____, an affiliate of _____. This will, undoubtedly, be a challenging situation,
and I look forward to moving to _____ with my wife within the next few months. We
plan to be there for approximately three years. As I had mentioned during our conversations
and in my resume, I am excited in being able to participate in the current developments in
central Europe.

I would like to extend my sincere thanks to you for your kind help and encouragement
during my job search. If I can be of any assistance to you in the future, please do not
hesitate to contact me. I was often reminded during the past few months that we too easily
lose contact with old friends. Let's try to stay in touch.

Until we find permanent living accommodations in _____, you can reach me either via
our home address (we plan to keep our house in New Jersey, and mail will be forwarded to
us), or at the office address (after January —th).

If you ever get a chance to visit _____, on business or pleasure, please be sure to let
me know.

Again, many thanks and best wishes.

Sincerely,

James Sharpe

James Sharpe

JS

POWER PHRASES

Consider using adaptations of these key phrases in your thank-you letters.

I am writing not only to share this good news with you but most importantly to thank you for your efforts on my behalf. If there is ever anything that I can do for you, please do not hesitate to call on me.

Thank you for all your help. I have accepted a position as a _____ for _____.

I want you to be among the first to know that my job search has come to a very successful conclusion.

I appreciate all the help and support you have provided over the last several months. It has made the job search process much easier for me. I look forward to staying in contact with you. Please let me know if I can be of any assistance to you in the future.

I would like to extend my sincere thanks to you for your kind help and encouragement during my job search. If I can be of any assistance to you in the future, please do not hesitate to contact me. I was often reminded during the past few months that we too easily loose contact with old friends. Let's try to stay in touch.

If you ever get a chance to visit _____, on business or pleasure, please be sure to let me know.

If there is ever anything I can do for you please call me. I hope you and your family have a wonderful holiday season and much luck and happiness in the new year.

Just a quick note to bring you up-to-date with what I am doing.

FOR MORE HELP

THE FOLLOWING INDIVIDUALS AND CORPORATIONS ARE LEADERS IN THEIR CHOSEN FIELDS. They each donated considerable time and energy to contributing to the quality of this book. They are the people on the firing line of the corporate hiring game. If you are a professional seeking professional career advice, you will be wise to seek advice from them. If they can't help you directly, they will point you in the right direction.

Banking

Melissa Webb, *Dunhill of Kalamazoo, Inc.*, 902 South Westnedge Avenue, Kalamazoo, MI 49008-1110, 616/381-3616, FAX: 616/381-2033.
Territory: National.
Specialization: Banking, Environmental Engineering.

Computers

Stanley Hart, *Hart Personnel Consultants*, 6340 Brookview Lane, West Bloomfield, MI 48322, 313/960-3555, FAX: 313/960-3556.
Territory: Metropolitan Detroit.
Specialization: Data Processing.

Fred Giuffrida, *Technical Search Services*, 618 Shoemaker Road, King of Prussia, PA 19406, 215/337-4420, FAX: 215/337-2297.
Territory: South Jersey, Philadelphia, Wilmington (DE).
Specialization: Computer, Data Processing.

Conrad Taylor, President, *Dotson Benefield, PDQS, Inc.*, 100 Crescent Center Parkway, Suite 300, Tucker, GA 30084, 404/493-1441, FAX: 404/493-7230.
Territory: Southeast US.
Specialization: Data Processing.

Jackie Beatty, *JMB Associates, Inc.*, 75 Foundry Street, Suite 34, South Easton, MA 02375, 508/238-0531.
Territory: National, Massachusetts.
Specialization: Computers, Software Engineering.

Patrice Moore, *Professional Solutions*, 440 Totten Pond Road, Waltham, MA 02154, 617/890-7900, FAX: 617/890-3736.
Territory: New England.
Specialization: MIS and Software Engineering.

Engineering

Charles Eibeler, *Amherst Personnel Group, Inc.*, 550 West Old Country Road, Hicksville, NY 11801, 516/433-7610, FAX: 516/433-7848.
Territory: National.
Specialization: Retail Sales and Office Services.

Cliff Horseman, *Cameron & Merrill Professional Search, Inc.*, 189 South Rogers Road, Suite 1624, Olathe, KS 66062, 913/782-0075, FAX: 913/780-4628, (residence) 913/894-4316.
Territory: National and International.
Specialization: Engineering, Environmental, Construction, Manufacturing, Legal, Banking.

Healthcare

Gary Snyder, *Fortune of Novi, Inc.*, 39555 Orchard Hill Place, Suite 225, Novi, MI 48375, 313/347-4800, FAX: 313/347-4085.
Territory: National.
Specialization: Healthcare, Engineering and Legal.

Bernard Ford, *Ford & Ford Search Consultants*, 105 Chestnut Street, Suite 34, Needham, MA 02192, 617/444-7335, FAX: 617/447-8200.
Territory: National.
Specialization: Health Care, Retail Sales and Human Resources.

Insurance

Jeff Hamilton, *Dunhill Professional Search, Inc.*, 2000 West Henderson Road, Suite 560, Columbus, OH 43220, 614/451-2664, FAX: 614/451-5129.
Territory: National.
Specialization: Insurance.

Office Support

Melissa Louer CPC, *Anton Wood Associates, Temp Force*, 1719 Central Avenue, Albany, NY 12205, 518/869-8477, FAX: 518/869-8567.
Territory: National.
Specialization: Support, Engineering.

General

Pat E. Goodwin CPC, Pauline Zanudio CPC, *Austin Career Consultants, Inc.*, 3624 N. Hills Drive, Suite 205, Austin, TX 78731, 512/346-6660, FAX: 512/346-6714.
Territory: National.
Specialization: Engineering, Data Processing, Accounting, Sales, Office Support, Temporary Placement.

Retail Sales

Rudy Thiessen, Director, Center of Career Management, *Price Waterhouse*, 1100-One Lombard Place, Winnipeg, Manitoba, Canada, 204/943-7321, FAX: 204/943-7774.
Territory: Province of Manitoba.
Specialization: Financial Management, General Management.

Sales

Joy J.D. Baldridge CPC, Staff VP, *Hipp Waters Inc.*, 209 Bedford Street, Stamford, CT 06901, 203/357-8400, FAX: 203/324-5819.
Territory: Metropolitan New York.
Specialization: Sales.

ALSO AVAILABLE
AT YOUR LOCAL BOOKSTORE

The JobBank Series
All JobBank books have now been expanded to include thousands of small businesses.

There are now 20 JobBank books, each covering a key U.S. job market with comprehensive and up-to-date information for every type of job-hunter. Each book is a complete research tool, providing the necessary guidance through every step of the job search, from career choice to the initial contact to the final follow-up letter.

In each book you'll find: full name, address, and telephone number of firm; contact for professional hiring; listings of common positions, educational backgrounds sought, and fringe benefits offered; sections on "The Basics of Job Winning" and "Resumes and Cover Letters," powerful complements to the rest of your research.

Books available:

The Atlanta JobBank
The Boston JobBank
The Carolina JobBank
The Chicago JobBank
The Dallas/Ft. Worth JobBank
The Denver JobBank
The Detroit JobBank
The Florida JobBank
The Houston JobBank
The Los Angeles JobBank
The Minneapolis/St. Paul JobBank
The New York JobBank
The Ohio JobBank
The Philadelphia JobBank
The Phoenix JobBank
The St. Louis JobBank
The San Francisco Bay Area JobBank
The Seattle JobBank
The Tennessee JobBank
The Metro Washington D.C. JobBank

If you cannot find our JobBank books at your bookstore, you may order them directly from the publisher.

BY PHONE: We accept Visa, Mastercard, and American Express. Call 1-800-USA-JOBS (in Massachusetts 617-767-8100). $3.75 will be added to your total order for shipping and handling.

BY MAIL: Write out the full title of the books you'd like to order and send payment, including $3.75 for shipping and handling (for the entire order), to: Bob Adams, Inc., 260 Center Street, Holbrook, MA 02343.

PLEASE CHECK AT YOUR LOCAL BOOKSTORE FIRST